STING OF THE HORNE

MCDONNELL DOUGLAS F/A-18 IN CANADIAN SERVICE

AETE's CF-18A, '701, carries a full air-to-ground war load of eight BL-755 cluster bombs. This test aircraft is fitted with a pitot boom on the nose and captive AIM-9 Sidewinder missiles on the wingtips. December 1983.

*THIS BOOK IS DEDICATED TO
FIGHTER PILOTS EVERYWHERE,
ESPECIALLY THOSE WHO NEVER
HAD TO GROW UP ...*

Acknowledgements

Managing Editor, Bob Baglow
Designed by Max McFadden
Reworked diagrams by Bob Migliardi
Photo retouching by John Matthews
Proofreading, Laurie Shubat
Typing and special assistance, Heather Bashow

Colour separations and film by Hadwen Graphics Ltd.,
Ottawa.
Printed and bound in Hong Kong by Scanner Arts

Originally published by Canuck Publications, 1987

Sole European trade distribution by:
Midland Counties Publications
24 The Hollow,
Earl Shilton, Leicester
England LE9 7NA
(tel. 0455-47256)

Aircraft line art by Bob Migliardi
Colour profile illustration by John Matthews

Copyright © Canuck Publications, 1987
Copyright© McClelland and Stewart, 1988

Canadian Cataloguing in Publication Data

Bashow, David L., 1946-
    Sting of the Hornet

ISBN 0-7710-1089-3

1. Hornet (Jet fighter plane). 2. Fighter planes – Canada.
I. Title.

UG1242.F5B38 1988   623.74'64'0971   C88-094347-5

Reprinted 1988 by

McClelland and Stewart
The Canadian Publishers
481 University Avenue
Toronto, Ontario
M5G 2E9

PREFACE 4

GENESIS OF A FIGHTER 5

IN THE BEGINNING 8

MEET THE HORNET 10

INTO SERVICE 30

LEARNING THE AIRCRAFT 32

FLIGHT PROFILE 34

SQUADRON COLOURS 40

PUTTING IT ALL TOGETHER 42

EUROPEAN OPERATIONS 46

SAFETY RECORD 54

HAPPENINGS 56

LOOKING AHEAD 66

SCALE DRAWINGS 69

GLOSSARY 72

CF-18 line view at Exercise William Tell '86 in Florida.

PREFACE

Sting of the Hornet seeks to record some of the activities and spirit of the first five years of Canadian CF-18 operations. The book is not intended to be an omnibus chronicle of the Hornet's service life. While every attempt has been made to portray events, systems and procedures as completely and accurately as possible, the manuscript will, by its very nature, be overtaken by events as the program evolves and matures.

Many generous written, verbal and material contributions were made by a host of people along the way. Assistance has ranged from the loan of photographs and drawings, to specific suggestions and a great deal of advice and practical encouragement, for which the author is extremely grateful.

Support was provided by many individuals within the Department of National Defence. At Cold Lake, these included LCol. Roy Riley, Maj. Gary Soule, Capts. Bob Wade, "Cash" Poulson and John Turner, artist Jim Belliveau, and Maj. Roy Rutledge and his staff of maintainers at 410 Sqn. In Base photo section, WO Marcotte, Sgt. Chaisson, MCpl. Beaudoin and Cpl. Theoret were particularly helpful on special projects.

A four-ship in stepped-up echelon left skim the cloud tops over southern Germany. The 330 US gallon centerline external fuel tank is a standard flight configuration.

The Alouettes of Bagotville have been in the vanguard of CF-18 operational activities in Canada during the phase-in process. We wish especially to cite skipper LCol. Jean-Michel Comtois, Capts. Frank Bergnach, Pierre Blais, Chris Hadfield and Pete Lang for their detailed inputs at a very busy time.

In the Ottawa area, LCol. John Croll (PMO), Capt. Dave Granger (DFS), Jim Baxter (DDDS), LS Jeff Charter (CADO Branch), Ray Gagnon (CNL Rockcliffe), WO Vic Johnson and Sgt. Tim Smith (DG Info.), deserve recognition. Capts. Rick Duchesneau and Louis Mackay at the Quebec Regional Information Office and Maj. Dave Kendall and his staff in the intelligence section of Fighter Group Headquarters in North Bay, completed the Canadian picture. In Europe, LCol. Ed McGillivray, LCol. Keith McDonald and Capt. Tom Sweeney proved invaluable in updating the author on Central European operations.

A special thank you is also due Mike Valenti, "Sunny" Pshebylo, "Turbo" Tarling, S. Woodend and Mr. R. Slaunwhite of McDonnell Douglas for a variety of important additions.

Effort has been made to verify names, places, units and dates, but inevitably errors will appear. For these, our apologies are sincerely tendered.

Dave Bashow
Bob Baglow

Ottawa, September 1987

GENESIS OF A FIGHTER

During the mid-1970s, the F/A-18 program for the US Navy and Marine Corps was evolving under a cloud of controversy and scepticism. The design challenge was great, for the aircraft was conceived as having a true multi-role capability, and touted by the manufacturers as the stand-alone replacement for a long-established attack aircraft, the A-7E Corsair, and the ubiquitous F-4 Phantom fighter.

The F/A-18's origins date from the Northrop P-530 Cobra, first unveiled to the public as a wooden mockup late in 1972. Deriving its nickname from the hooded appearance created by the LEX, or leading edge extension, the Cobra became a living, air-breathing reality in 1973 when it was redesignated the YF-17, and nominated along with General Dynamics' YF-16 as a finalist in the USAF lightweight air superiority fighter program. Although the YF-16 went on to win that flyoff, Northrop's prototype was revamped and revitalized in cooperation with McDonnell Douglas, a company experienced in the specialized requirements of carrier-based fighters. The U.S. Navy demanded an aircraft not only with the F-16's superb close-in dog-fighting characteristics, but one that could easily be converted to carry the medium range all-weather AIM-7 Sparrow missile, and adapted to the attack role. Increased safety afforded by twin engines was also a very attractive factor to the USN, flying the vast majority of their missions far out to sea and beyond gliding distance from land in the event of a serious emergency.

The USN announced the F/A-18 as their choice for a new fighter/attack aircraft on May 2, 1975. McDonnell Douglas, Saint Louis (McAir) became the main contractor with Northrop Corporation in California as subcontractor, construction workload being shared approximately 60/40. Northrop would construct the vertical tail assemblies, the center and aft fuselage portions, while McAir was to build the rest of the airframe structure and wings, then bring all components together in final assembly. This was a sizeable contract,

Three 409 Sqn. CF-18s thunder over the picturesque landscape of the Bavarian Alps on a low-level training flight. The leading edge strakes, which blend the wing into the fuselage and are responsible for the creation of a significant amount of lift, show off to good advantage in this photograph.

consisting of 1,366 jet fighters for the USN and an additional 144 for the USMC.

Since the F/A-18 was destined to be much heavier than was originally intended with the YF-17, due to Navy requirements, there was an obvious need for more thrust. This deficiency was rectified by the adoption of General Electric's F-404 engine, an enhanced and uprated version of the YF-17's YJ-101 powerplant. In order to provide an all-weather capability, provision was made for Sparrow missiles, along with a suitable multi-mode radar, a compatible fire control system and appropriate avionics for the all-weather attack role. Enlargement of the nose to accommodate the Hughes APG-65 radar was also necessary. Naval operations demanded greater range capabilities, so internal fuel capacity was increased by nearly two-thirds, to 9,860 pounds. Additional external fuel could also be carried in wing pylon and fuselage centreline drop tanks, and provision was made for air-to-air refuelling.

The high impact forces of carrier operations entailed considerable "beefing up" of undercarriage members, as well as additional structural reinforcement throughout the aircraft. Wing area was increased by 50 square feet and the span by 2.5 feet along with extension of the wing chord. The LEX, which aerodynamically fairs the

AETE CF-18B 188907, salvos a pod of nineteen stock 2.75" rockets over the Primrose Lake evaluation range.

wings to the fuselage and creates a considerable amount of lift in the bargain, was refined and increased in size, and aerodynamic improvements were made to leading and trailing edge flaps, ailerons and the horizontal stabilators.

High purchase costs demanded a long, useful service career, an airframe life of 6,000 flight hours, extreme ease of maintenance and rapid turn-around capability. Since the aircraft had been envisaged from the outset as a single-seater, a great

deal of design emphasis was placed on the "user friendliness" of cockpit instrumentation. Much use was made of both CRT (cathode ray tube) and HOTAS (hands-on-throttle-and-stick) technology pioneered in the F-15 Eagle to minimize pilot workload. The result has been highly successful.

November 1978 marked the date of the first F/A-18 flight and almost exactly two years later in November 1980, the USN commissioned its first F/A-18 training squadron at NAS Lemoore, California.

A tactical target receives the full treatment from high-velocity CRV-7 2.75" rockets. Compare the increased kinetic energy of the rocket motor burn, along with the dense white smoke trail, over the earlier variant shown in the photograph on the facing page.

IN THE BEGINNING

Early doubt and criticism surrounding the US F/A-18 program was due largely to USAF rejection of the basic aircraft type (YF-17) and to numerous "teething troubles" during the test and development stage — problems that were all eventually corrected. Replacement of two aircraft types in widely divergent roles by the F/A-18, unproven for either role, was meeting major and continuous opposition. The Canadian requirement was no less formidable, as the aircraft chosen as Canada's New Fighter Aircraft (NFA) would ultimately have to replace both the CF-104 Starfighter and CF-5 Freedom Fighter in surface attack roles, and the venerable CF-101 Voodoo in the air defence role. Throughout the late 1970s, interested Canadians watched intently as USN/USMC F/A-18 implementation plans progressed.

In Canada the primary NORAD mission would be the air defence of North America and adjacent maritime zones. Within NATO a very wide range of tasks would prevail, including interception, aerial combat, forward air defence operations, low level combat air patrol (CAP), AWACS defence, mixed fighter force duties, fighter sweep and escort, long range attacks on enemy airfields and aircraft on the ground, and support of friendly troops in the battlefield.

What led specifically to Canada's selection of the CF-18 as the New Fighter Aircraft? In March 1977, the Canadian Cabinet authorized the Department of National Defence to obtain proposals from industry for the acquisition of approximately 130 to 150 aircraft. The high performance, multi-role fighter acquired was to be:

1. An "off-the-shelf" buy, with an absolute minimum of Canadian-unique features;
2. Purchased within a fixed budget of $2.34 billion in August 1977 dollars; and
3. Capable of providing considerable industrial offset benefits to Canada.

In September, a formal Request for Proposal was issued to six contractors concerning seven aircraft, and a detailed evaluation of all candidates was carried out by the NFA Project Office. Based on their recommendations, in November, 1978, Cabinet selected a short list of contenders — the General Dynamics F-16 Falcon and the McDonnell Douglas F/A-18 Hornet. After further detailed evaluation, the latter one was chosen in April 1980 with an initial contract purchase of 138 aircraft, the first arriving October 1982.

Not only was the Hornet the logical choice for its designated missions, but its inherent growth potential and current capabilities should enable it to effectively counter any adversary into the next century. Two-engine reliability is considered an absolute requirement for high-speed low-level operations in central Europe where, in the CF-104 era, a birdstrike frequently resulted in catastrophic engine failure and, at best, in the pilot "walking home." The aircraft is also an excellent air-to-air refuelling platform, capable of receiving a full load of fuel in just a few minutes. This additional feature would allow non-stop CF-18 trans-Atlantic deployment directly to an active theatre of operations, should the need arise.

The design also incorporates a host of innovative features, such as advanced cockpit controls and displays, extensive use of carbon-epoxy composite materials, a digital fly-by-wire flight control system and multi-mode radar, all of which represent the latest in technology.

CF-18 '901 was the first production aircraft delivered. A special electronic pod on the port wingtip provides position inputs and firing cues to the electronic Air Combat Maneuvering Range. Those inputs are then used later as a debriefing tool, providing an accurate reconstruction of events during the mission.

First of 138. CF-18 '901 on rollout at the McDonnell Douglas plant in St. Louis, Missouri, October 1982. Production breakdown calls for 98 CF-18As and 40 CF-18Bs.

MEET THE HORNET

The CF-18 is 56 feet of sleek, grey lethality. The variable camber wings have hydraulically actuated leading and trailing edge flaps and ailerons. Twin stabilizers are angled outboard 20° from the vertical and the twin rudders and differential stabilators are also hydraulically actuated. A speed brake is mounted atop the aft fuselage between the vertical stabilizers.

Locomotion is provided by two General Electric F404-GE-400 low bypass, axial-flow turbofan engines with afterburning. 10,700 pounds of military thrust from each engine, and maximum afterburner thrust rated at nearly 16,000 pounds, deliver performance that places the Hornet in the 1-to-1 thrust-to-weight ratio category — a very meaningful factor to a fighter pilot. Diminutive beside engines of comparable power output, the F404 is a striking example of the advances in engine technology over the last 20 years. While achieving similar thrust, the F404 is barely half the weight and two-thirds the length of the J79, which until recently was a jet engine mainstay in the Western world powering the CF-104 Starfighter and F-4 Phantom, among others. In addition, the total number of engine components has been reduced by at least a third over the J79, accruing additional weight savings and improved engine simplicity. The F404 is a fuel miser, showing disdain for the gas-gulping greed of its J79 predecessor. Specific fuel consumption rate is much lower, which translates into increased combat effectiveness in terms of range and endurance for "the guy behind the pole." Along with these obvious gains in performance, the engine was designed in seven separate modules for ease of maintenance.

The result — engine technicians swear *by* the F404, not *at* it!

The Hornet displays many innovative features, some of which stem from its USN nautical heritage. For example, the wing fold system which was designed for optimum storage on carriers also allows maintenance crews to hangar CF-18s a great deal more efficiently.

Flight Controls
One of the CF-18's high-technology marvels is its flight control system, which provides excellent stability and handling

An engine pull at Cold Lake, August 1985.

characteristics throughout the entire flight envelope. Two digital Flight Control Computers (FCCs) provide a four-channel, redundant fly-by-wire system controlling the ailerons, differential horizontal stabilators, differential leading edge/trailing edge flaps and twin rudders. Normally, inputs

Air-to-air refuelling is an essential tactical requirement. Here, two CF-18Bs prepare to engage their CC-137 (Boeing 707) tanker for a "big gulp".

12

to the hydraulic actuators are provided by the two FCCs through the full authority Control Augmentation System (CAS). A Direct Electrical Link (DEL) mode automatically backs up the CAS. DEL is normally a digital system but has an analog mode for backup aileron and rudder control. If DEL fails, a mechanical link (MECH mode) automatically provides roll and pitch control through a direct mechanical input from the stick to the stabilator actuators. MECH mode bypasses both flight control computers and the stabilator actuator servo valves. Multiple redundant

paths ensure that single failures have little or no effect on control. Multiple failures are almost unheard of but when they *do* occur, things can get rather "sporty." More on that later...

The flap system also provides a great deal of versatility. A three-position flap switch (AUTO, HALF, FULL) on the lower left instrument panel selects which of two

Landing gear and flaps fully extended, Capt. Don Thornton makes his final approach over the Rhine Valley heading for home base at CFB Baden-Soellingen. August 13, 1987.

flight control computer modes (AUTO FLAP UP or TAKEOFF AND LAND) is active.

With flaps HALF or FULL, there is high stability in roll, pitch and yaw and a positive stick force has to be held in order to fly at other than the trimmed Angle of Attack (AOA). Precise control of AOA is the net result, and this helps in flying an accurate final approach. With the flaps selected to AUTO, they combine with ailerons, stabilators and rudders to become part of the primary flight control system, automatically programming up and down in response to whatever flight conditions are encountered. Unlike TAKEOFF AND LAND mode, in AUTO the aircraft is trimmed to a steady-state 1g flight, and manual trimming is not required in pitch.

Cockpit Checkout

At the leading edge of a complex avionic system is the high technology cockpit, designed from the outset to minimize pilot workload. It is dominated by three large 5" x 5" cathode ray tubes called Digital Display Indicators, or DDIs. Left and right DDIs are physically and functionally interchangeable and display a wealth of information, including systems status, checklist procedures, engine performance parameters, radar control, weapons and sensor information. The lower DDI, called the horizontal indicator (HI), is reserved for navigation information and the moving map display. Heart of the aircraft avionics is the mission computer system consisting of two high speed, stored-program, general purpose programmable digital computers with core

High technology exemplified. The moving map display is on the centre HI, the right DDI shows HUD information, and the left DDI is turned off.

memory (affectionately known as "Spock 1" and "Spock 2"). The pilot normally "talks" to them through the Up Front Controller (UFC), a centrally located panel flanked by the DDIs, or through a host of grey pushbuttons that ring the three displays.

The UFC comprises master controls for two UHF/VHF radios (both AM and FM), TACAN, ILS, VOR, ADF, IFF, and autopilot, and a keyboard for entry of frequencies, waypoint data and weapons programs. Looking out the front windscreen, a large and very comprehensive Head Up Display (HUD) optically focused to infinity dominates without intruding on visibility.

The HUD provides all essential flight information such as aircraft speed, altitude, attitude and trends, as well as a *lot* of tactical information for the pilot, including radar warning threats (indications of external radar systems tracking his aircraft), thus negating the need to look continuously inside at cockpit displays. In fact, the HUD is the most important instrument during nearly all phases of flight, and has revolutionized procedures such as the traditional "head down" time-honoured form of instrument flying.

The AN/ASM-130 inertial navigation system is a self-contained fully automatic dead reckoning navigation system. The INS detects aircraft motion and provides acceleration, present position, velocity, roll, pitch and true heading to related systems. Correction signals from aircraft accelerometers provide constant levelling. Both periodic and pilot-initiated Built-In-Test (BIT) checks are used by the INS.

The main navigation display indicator is the HI, which contains a full-colour Moving Map Display (MMD) and is overlaid with representative navigational information. Navigation information can also be displayed on the HUD, and full HUD symbology can be called up on either the left or right DDIs.

Upfront control panel.

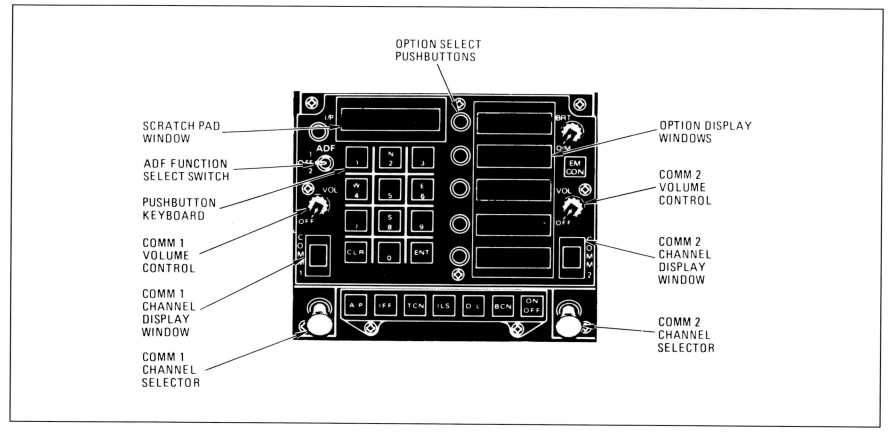

15

Navigation controls and indicators

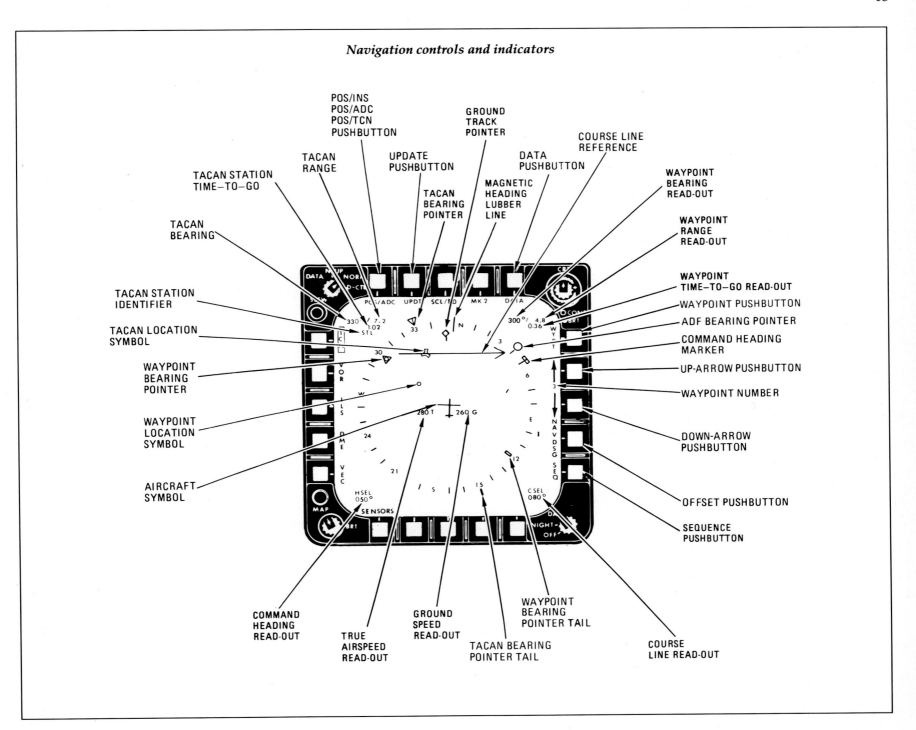

The sub-arctic tundra forms a very Canadian backdrop for this Cold Lake-based aircraft. An ACMR instrumentation pod may be seen on the port wingtip and a captive Sidewinder missile seeker head assembly on the starboard tip.

Weapons Control and Delivery

The Hornet's weapons system is programmed to be in one of three operational states during flight as determined by master mode selections.

Navigation

NAV mode is primarily designed to keep track of the present aircraft position and determine a course to another destination. The primary navigation component is the INS, which provides a grid reference (latitude, longitude and altitude) as well as attitude data, which the mission computer uses in various navigation and weapon delivery computations.

Air-to-Air

When the A/A master mode is selected, the weapons system is configured to detect and attack airborne targets. The mission computer configures the radar search parameters and indicator displays to be compatible with weapons selection. Target data from the radar is acquired and the following tasks are performed:

1. Detects airborne targets for attack;
2. Tracks single targets or provides up to 10 multiple target tracks (displays up to 8 targets);
3. Makes threat assessments for target priority assignments;
4. Computes weapon delivery parameters;
5. Prepares air-to-air missiles for launch; and
6. Routes pilot-initiated weapon launch and firing signals to the selected weapons.

Air-to-Ground

Selection of the A/G master mode shifts system attention to the detection and attack of ground targets and related functions:

1. Detects ground targets for attack;
2. Tracks fixed or moving ground targets for weapon delivery computations;
3. Prepares air-to-ground missiles (if available) for launch;
4. Delivers bombs automatically with pilot consent at the computed release point; and
5. Routes pilot-initiated weapons launch/release firing signals to manually delivered weapons.

The CF-18 has nine external armament stations for air-to-air and air-to-ground weapons, as well as an internally mounted M61 six-barrel 20mm cannon capable of selectable firing rates of either 6,000 or 4,000 rounds per minute. Stations 1 and 9 (left and right wingtips) are AIM-9 Sidewinder heat-seeking missile positions, while stations 4 and 6 (left and right fuselage) are designated AIM-7 Sparrow radar-guided missile locations. Other hard points may also carry both Sparrow and Sidewinder, as well as a myriad of conventional and laser-guided bombs, cluster bombs, 2.75" rockets, training weapons and numerous air-to-surface missiles.

Versatile Radar

Perhaps the single most vital piece of equipment is the mighty Hughes AN/APG-65 multiple mode search-and-track radar.

Air-to-Air Modes

Detected airborne targets are tracked in range, velocity and angle by locking-on to the return echo and monitoring echo delay time, carrier frequency Doppler shift and angular position. Target track data is supplied to the mission computer for weapon attack computations by solving the intercept problem and providing attack symbology on the HUD for either an air-to-air missile or gun attack.

On a typically overcast European day, Capt. Doug Stroud banks his aircraft to show off its configuration: four LAU-5003 rocket pods and three 330 US gallon external fuel tanks. Baden, August 18, 1987.

The **Velocity Search (VS)** mode provides superior long-range capability for detecting nose aspect targets in the look-down regime. The **Range While Search (RWS)** mode uses both high and medium Pulse Repetition Frequency (PRF) waveforms to detect targets at any and all aspects and relative velocities out to about 80 nautical miles. **Track While Scan (TWS)** is a high, medium or interleaved PRF mode which may be used during the closing phase of an attack at ranges inside 40 nautical miles. It maintains files on up to ten separate targets and displays information on the eight highest priority ones to the pilot in terms of relative threat. **Single Target Track (STT)** mode can be entered automatically or manually from any of the described search modes. It is the primary method of tracking a target during weapons employment phase. In STT, the radar is capable of tracking the target through most maneuvers and provides attack steering commands and shoot cues for both Sparrow and Sidewinder on the HUD. **Raid Assessment (RA)** mode breaks out or "sorts" the relative positions of enemy aircraft flying in close formations, and is effective at ranges out to 30 nautical miles. This mode uses Doppler beam sharpening techniques based on expanding the area around a single target return to give increased resolution and subsequently the capability to break out the individual components of a formation.

Switchology

A pilot normally selects the radar display on the right DDI, and radar functions can be chosen by surrounding push-

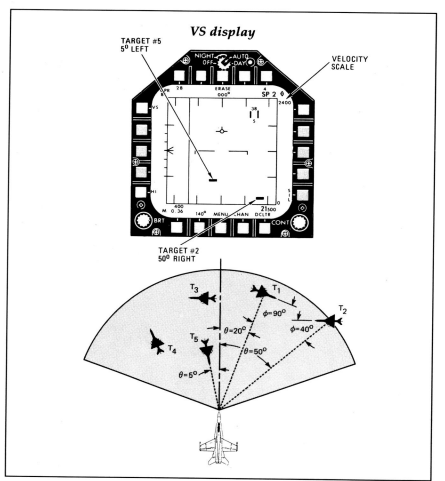

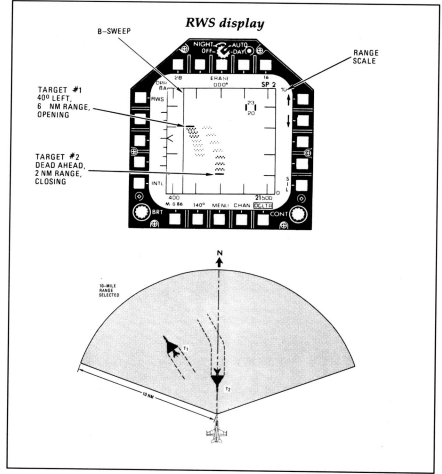

buttons or the Hands-on-Throttle-and-Stick (HOTAS) controls, where the hands are resting to control the aircraft. The **Throttle Designator Control (TDC)** is a two-axis positioning device with a momentary pushbutton switch, providing slewing control for various items depending on HUD/radar selection. The **sensor control switch** has several functions both in A/A and in A/G modes, but in the former, it selects the ACM automatic target acquisition modes and initializes the HUD and radar displays accordingly. The

radar automatically locks-on to the first target which flies into the selected field of view, which is different for each position of the sensor switch.

The APG-65 employs four automatic acquisition modes with the sensor control switch and a fifth by selecting gun acquisition mode. Boresight (BST), wide acquisition (WACQ), automatic acquisition (AACQ), vertical acquisition (VACQ), and gun acquisition (GUN), search predetermined, different areas of space, and attempt to lock-on to the first target detect-

ed within their respective envelopes. If the wrong target is acquired, the system can be "bumped" or re-selected. The dimensions and angular limits of the sweeps of these automatic modes, which bypass time-critical manual acquisition procedures, vary depending on needs such as the intensity of maneuvering required to track the target.

The **weapon select switch** commands the weapons system, consisting of the radar, armament and displays to the air-to-air mode, and chooses a particular

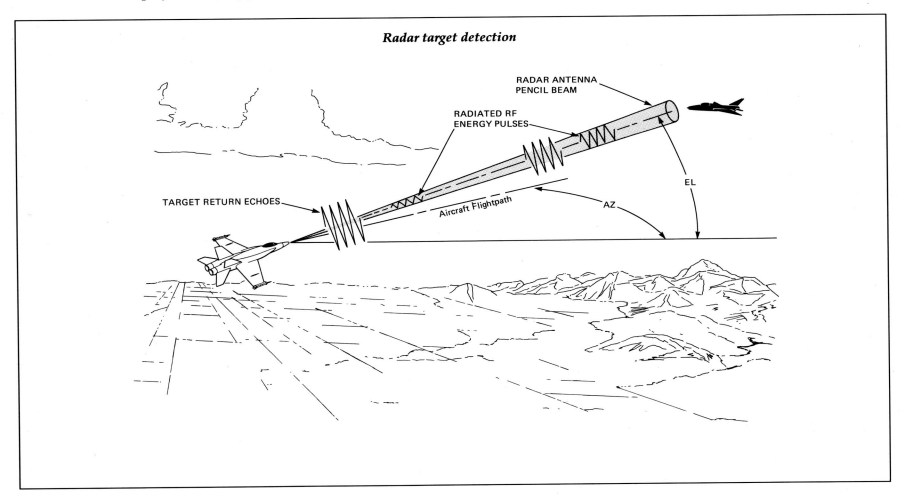

Radar target detection

RADAR ANTENNA
PENCIL BEAM

RADIATED RF
ENERGY PULSES

TARGET RETURN ECHOES

Aircraft Flightpath

EL

AZ

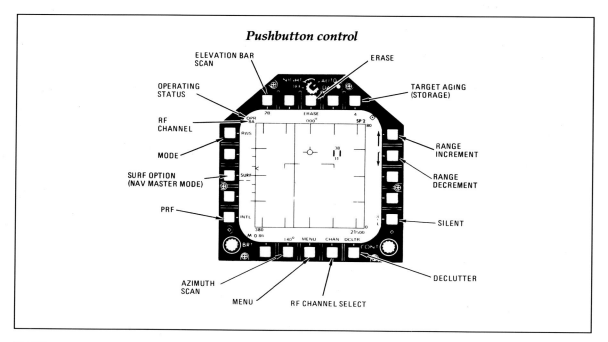

Pushbutton control

ELEVATION BAR SCAN

ERASE

OPERATING STATUS

TARGET AGING (STORAGE)

RF CHANNEL

MODE

RANGE INCREMENT

SURF OPTION (NAV MASTER MODE)

RANGE DECREMENT

PRF

SILENT

AZIMUTH SCAN

DECLUTTER

MENU

RF CHANNEL SELECT

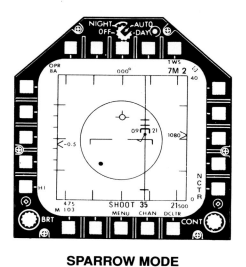

SPARROW MODE

HOTAS controls

THROTTLES

RAID SELECT BUTTON

RADAR ANTENNA ELEVATION CONTROL

TDC

SP (FORWARD)

GUN (AFT)

SW (DOWN)

CONTROL STICK

SENSOR CONTROL SWITCH

WEAPON SELECT SWITCH

UNDESIGNATE BUTTON

SENSOR CONTROL SWITCH FUNCTIONS

BST (FORWARD)

WACQ (LEFT)

AACQ (RIGHT)

VACQ (AFT)

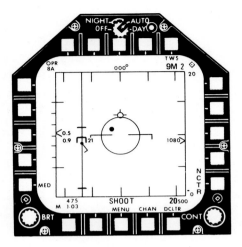

SIDEWINDER MODE

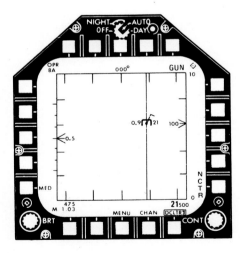

GUN MODE

Summary of Air-to-Air Modes

Mode	Function	Description
Velocity Search (VS)	Long range target search	High pulse repetition frequencies (HPRF) are employed to provide a high energy level for long range target detection in the clutter free velocity spectrum (nose aspect targets).
Range While Search (RWS)	All aspect target search	HPRF and medum PRF (MPRF) are interleaved to provide both nose and tail aspect target detection. MPRF also enables target ranging.
Single Target Track (STT)	A/A weapon delivery	Radar continuously measures target position, enabling accurate computations for a missile intercept or gun fire hit.
Track While Scan (TWS)	Multiple target evaluation	TWS provides simultaneous track and display of multiple targets. Target track displays include the respective target aspect angle pointers and priority assignments.
Raid Assessment (RAID)	High resolution detection	RAID mode is entered from STT or TWS and provides high resolution of the small airspace about the tracked target. Expanded display enables determination of number of targets in formation beyond visual range and their position relative to tracked target.
ACM Modes: BST (boresight) WACQ (wide acquisition) VACQ (vertical acquisition) AACQ (automatic acquisition) GUN (gun acquisition)	Rapid acquisition and track of close range targets	ACM modes bypass time consuming manual target acquisition procedures and enable immediate control of a close range threat.

Air-to-air attack displays with
respective HUD symbology

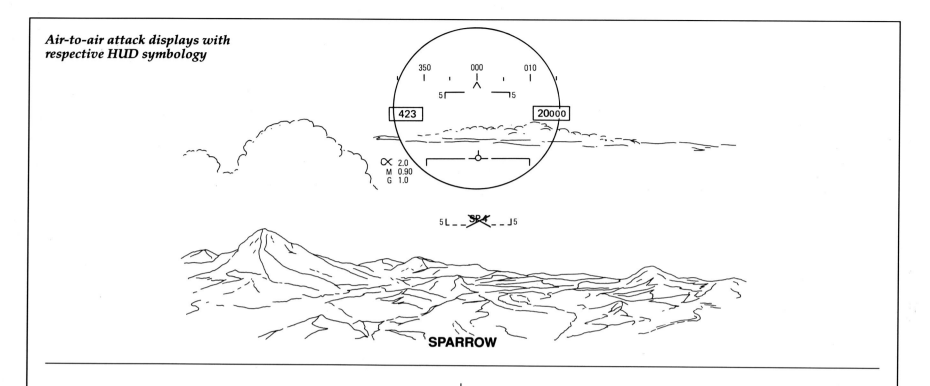

SPARROW

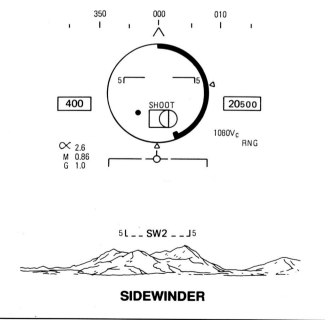

SIDEWINDER

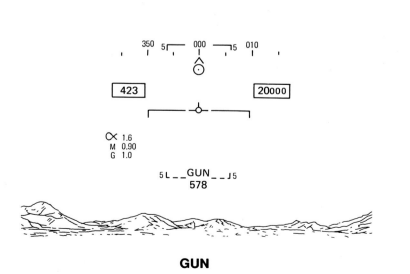

GUN

Air-to-Ground radar function modes

Mode	Function	Description
Real Beam Ground Map (MAP)	Display of terrain features	Provides a large area map and assists in navigation and location of surface targets.
Sea Surface Search (SEA)	Detection of discrete surface targets	The radar provides high sensitivity for detecting discrete surface targets while minimizing diffuse clutter (sea returns). The radar also guards against sidelobe land returns.
Ground Moving Target Indications (GMT)	Detection of moving ground targets	Moving targets are highlighted. (trucks, tanks)
Terrain Avoidance (TA)	Detection of terrain protrusions	Two levels of protruding terrain are displayed in addition to weather indications. Enables extremely low level navigation (flying valleys) en route to a target.
Precision Velocity Update (PVU)	Accurate aircraft groundspeed	PVU is automatically selected at specific intervals and provides an accurate groundspeed measurement to the MC. Enables precise navigation and aircraft position information.
Air-to-Ground Ranging (AGR)	Slant range measurements	Radar provides an accurate slant measurement to the designated ground target enabling accurate weapon delivery computations.
Fixed Target Track (FTT)	Automatic track of ground targets	Enables precise navigation to a target and computation of a weapon release point.
Ground Moving Target Track (GMTT)	Automatic track of a moving surface target	Enables precise navigation to a moving target and computation of a weapon release point.

armament depending on switch position: forward for Sparrow missiles; down — Sidewinders; and aft — guns. The pilot can instantly direct his weapon system to any air-to-air armament, an extremely useful (and life-prolonging) capability should he be bounced while engaged in an air-to-ground weapon delivery.

Air-to-Ground Modes

For A/G functions, the mission computer integrates data inputs from the INS, the Air Data Computer (ADC) and the radar to compute velocity and position relative to the target for navigation and weapon delivery problems. The computer then outputs the proper aiming symbols on the HUD, the release commands in the computed delivery modes, the automatic centering of a weapons "stick" (multiple drop) on target and the release commands to deploy weapons at the selected interval.

In the **AUTO** mode, command steering is provided to an appropriate weapon release point for a bomb drop on a designated target. Ordnance is automatically released with pilot consent at the proper time for a target hit. The mission computer presents an Azimuth Steering Line (ASL) on the HUD and the pilot follows command steering while executing the appropriate weapon delivery maneuver by holding the HUD velocity vector on the ASL. This steering command will guide the Hornet to pass the bottom end of the selected weapon flightpath profile over the target.

Flight Director (FD) mode is comparable to AUTO, but also provides command steering to intercept a predetermined attack course. Both AUTO and FD can be coupled to the autopilot for azimuth steering.

LEFT CONSOLE

1. FIRE TEST PANEL
2. GROUND POWER PANEL
3. THROTTLE QUADRANT
4. EXTERIOR LIGHTS PANEL
5. FUEL PANEL
6. FLIGHT CONTROL SYSTEM PANEL
7. COMMUNICATION PANEL
8. LIQUID OXYGEN QUANTITY INDICATOR
9. ANTI-G VALVE
10. PILOT SERVICES PANEL
    - ANTI-G
    - SUIT VENT
    - OXYGEN
11. COMMUNICATION CONNECTION
12. MISSION COMPUTER AND HYDRAULIC ISOLATE PANEL
13. ANTENNA SELECT PANEL
14. AUXILIARY POWER UNIT PANEL
15. GENERATOR TIE CONTROL SWITCH (some aircraft)
16. ECM DISPENSER BUTTON
17. GROUND POWER DECAL
18. LEFT ESSENTIAL CIRCUIT BREAKERS
19. CANOPY MANUAL HANDLE AND DRIVE
20. NUCLEAR WEAPON SWITCH

NOTE

RADIO OVERRIDE SWITCH ON CF 18B AIRCRAFT ONLY

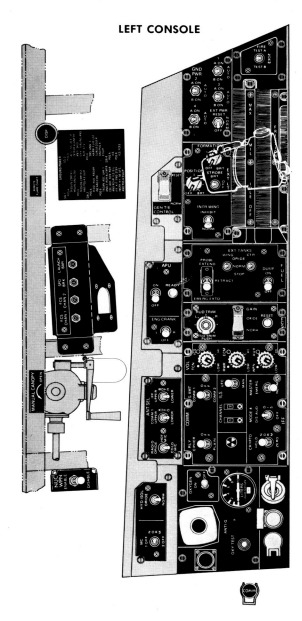

INSTRUMENT PANEL

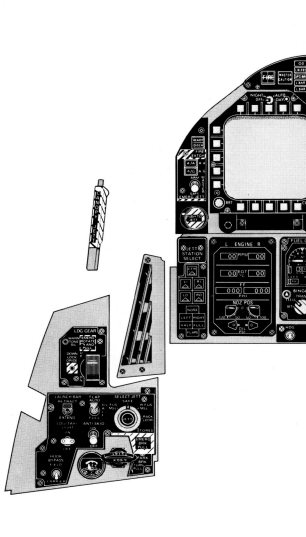

1. LOCK SHOOT LIGHTS
2. HEAD-UP DISPLAY (HUD)
3. ANGLE-OF-ATTACK INDEXER LIGHTS
4. LEFT ENGINE FIRE WARNING/EXTINGUISHER LIGHT
5. MASTER CAUTION LIGHT
6. LEFT WARNING/CAUTION/ADVISORY LIGHTS
7. HUD VIDEO CAMERA CONTROL
8. RIGHT WARNING/CAUTION/ADVISORY LIGHTS
9. AUXILIARY POWER UNIT FIRE WARNING/EXTINGUISHER LIGHT
10. RIGHT ENGINE FIRE WARNING/EXTINGUISHER LIGHT
11. CANOPY INTERNAL JETTISON HANDLE
12. MASTER ARM PANEL
13. LEFT DIGITAL DISPLAY INDICATOR (DDI)
14. UPFRONT CONTROL PANEL
15. RIGHT DIGITAL DISPLAY INDICATOR (DDI)
16. MAP GAIN/SPIN RECOVERY PANEL
17. EMERGENCY JETTISON BUTTON
18. HUD CONTROL
19. STANDBY MAGNETIC COMPASS
20. STATION JETTISON SELECT
21. LANDING GEAR AND FLAP POSITION LIGHTS
22. ENGINE MONITOR INDICATOR
    - L & R RPM
    - L & R EGT
    - L & R FUEL FLOW
    - L & R NOZZLE POSITION
    - L & R OIL PRESSURE
23. FUEL QUANTITY INDICATOR
24. HEADING AND COURSE SET SWITCHES
25. HORIZONTAL INDICATOR (HI)
26. STANDBY ATTITUDE INDICATOR
27. BLANK PANEL
28. STANDBY AIRSPEED INDICATOR

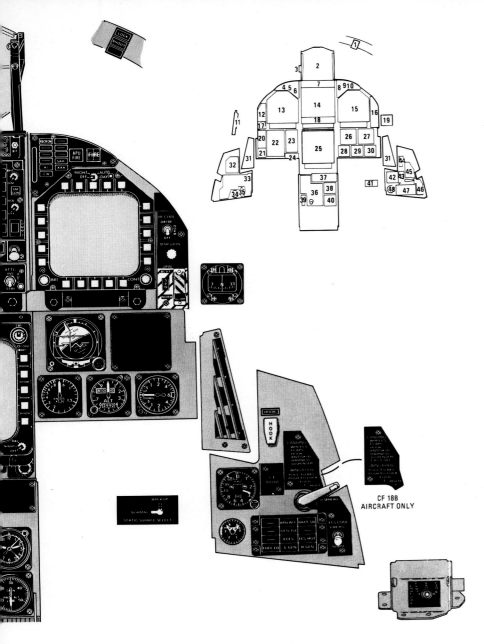

CF 18B
AIRCRAFT ONLY

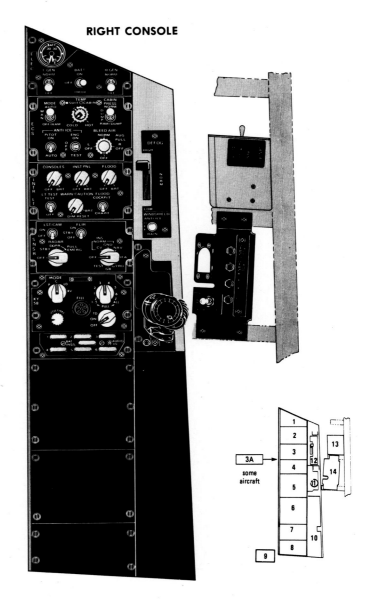

3A →
some
aircraft

29. STANDBY ALTIMETER
30. STANDBY RATE OF CLIMB INDICATOR
31. ENVIRONMENT CONTROL LOUVRES
32. LANDING GEAR HANDLE AND WARNING TONE
    SILENCE BUTTON
33. SELECT JETTISON BUTTON
34. BRAKE ACCUMULATOR PRESSURE GAUGE
35. EMERGENCY AND PARKING BRAKE HANDLE
36. DISPENSER/ECM PANEL
37. BLANK PANEL
38. CLOCK

39. RUDDER PEDAL ADJUST LEVER
40. COCKPIT ALTIMETER
41. STATIC SOURCE SELECT
42. RADAR ALTIMETER
43. AIRCRAFT BUREAU NUMBER
44. ARRESTING HOOK HANDLE AND LIGHT
45. LANDING CHECK LIST AND WING FOLD SWITCH
46. FLIGHT COMPUTER COOL SWITCH
47. CAUTION LIGHTS PANEL
48. HYD 1 AND HYD 2 PRESSURE INDICATOR

1. ELECTRICAL POWER PANEL
2. ENVIRONMENT CONTROL SYSTEM PANEL
3. INTERIOR LIGHTS PANEL
3A. BLANK PANEL (some aircraft)
    (not shown)
4. SENSOR PANEL
5. KY-58 CONTROL
6. BLANK PANEL
7. BLANK PANEL
8. BLANK PANEL
9. FAN TEST SWITCH
10. MAP AND DATA CASE
11. UTILITY LIGHT
12. DEFOG PANEL
13. INTERNAL CANOPY SWITCH
14. RIGHT ESSENTIAL CIRCUIT BREAKERS

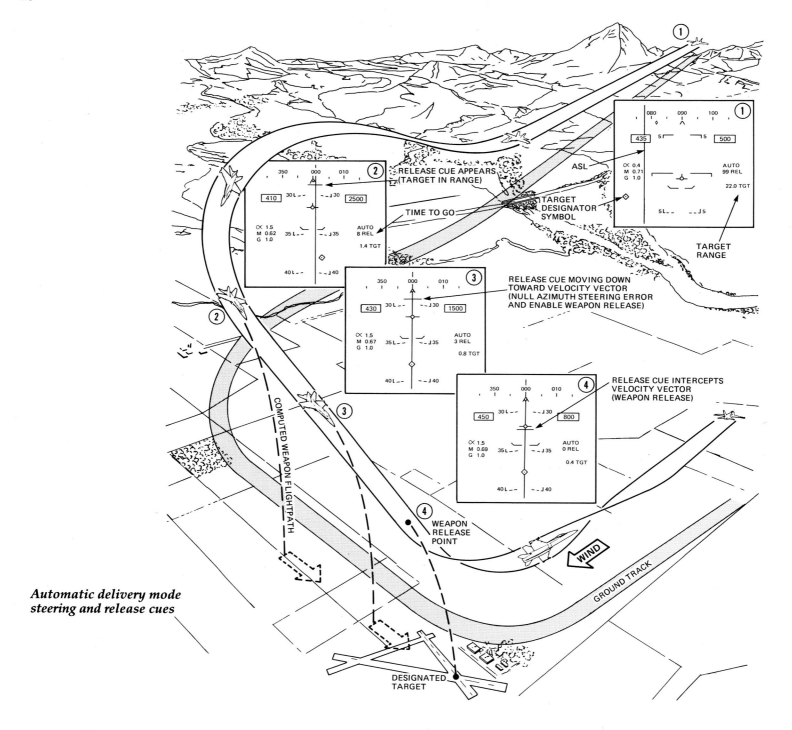

1

080   090   100

435   5 ⌐   ⌐ 5   500

∝ 0.4
M 0.71
G 1.0

AUTO
99 REL

22.0 TGT

5 L⌐   ⌐⌐ J 5

TARGET
RANGE

2

350   000   010

410   30 L⌐   ⌐⌐ J 30   2500

∝ 1.5
M 0.62
G 1.0

35 L⌐   ⌐⌐ J 35

AUTO
8 REL

1.4 TGT

40 L⌐   ⌐⌐ J 40

RELEASE CUE APPEARS
(TARGET IN RANGE)

ASL

TARGET
DESIGNATOR
SYMBOL

TIME TO GO

3

350   000   010

430   30 L⌐   ⌐⌐ J 30   1500

∝ 1.5
M 0.67
G 1.0

35 L⌐   ⌐⌐ J 35

AUTO
3 REL

0.8 TGT

40 L⌐   ⌐⌐ J 40

RELEASE CUE MOVING DOWN
TOWARD VELOCITY VECTOR
(NULL AZIMUTH STEERING ERROR
AND ENABLE WEAPON RELEASE)

4

350   000   010

450   30 L⌐   ⌐⌐ J 30   800

∝ 1.5
M 0.69
G 1.0

35 L⌐   ⌐⌐ J 35

AUTO
0 REL

0.4 TGT

40 L⌐   ⌐⌐ J 40

RELEASE CUE INTERCEPTS
VELOCITY VECTOR
(WEAPON RELEASE)

COMPUTED WEAPON FLIGHTPATH

WEAPON
RELEASE
POINT

WIND

GROUND TRACK

DESIGNATED
TARGET

*Automatic delivery mode
steering and release cues*

The **Continuously Computed Impact Point (CCIP)** mode of bomb delivery is very similar to the AUTO solution, except that no command steering is provided because no specific target has been designated. Impact point for the selected weapon is continuously displayed on the HUD (bottom of the weapon flightpath profile). The pilot flies the aircraft to steer the impact symbol (CCIP cross) across the target and manually initiates weapon release by activating the bomb release "pickle" button. A Displayed Impact Line (DIL) is also shown on the HUD, which serves as a guide for steering the CCIP cross to the target.

Of course, the Hornet is not solely dependent upon electronic wizardry; there is a manual bombing mode as well, just in case "the magic" is having an off-day. **(MAN)** mode provides a back-up visual delivery capability and is selected automatically by the aircraft under some failure conditions or manually by the pilot at any time desired. The pilot then maneuvers the aircraft to position the HUD reticle on target, just like the good old days.

The APG-65 displays potent capabilities for radar navigation as well. There are modes for navigating to the target area, searching land or sea surfaces, providing a detailed map of terrain and tracking fixed or moving targets (for details see chart on p. 23). In the ground mapping modes, since the radar returns are artificially processed they are much more realistic and require far less interpretation than is the case with more primitive radars. In all modes, the display is computer-adjusted to present the map from a vertical or "God's eye" vantage point, rather than the shallow angle obtained from an aircraft's flight path, which would give a distorted view making recognition of ground features more difficult.

CCIP delivery mode cues.

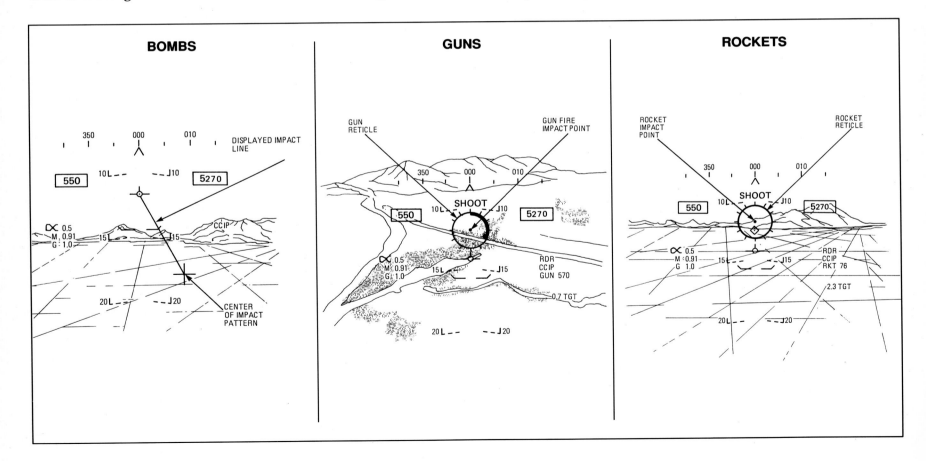

EXPAND options are limited to maximum ranges of 40 nautical miles, and may be thought of as using Doppler Beam Sharpening (DBS) techniques to provide a "zoom" detail capability in MAP mode for sectors (EXP1), patches (EXP2) and the still more specific sub-patches (EXP3).

Terrain Avoidance (TA) mode searches the area ahead of the aircraft and displays detected obstructions on the radar scope. The antenna scan is limited to +/-35° centered on the aircraft ground track, and the radar searches out to 10 nautical miles. Clearance plane templates are then projected on the display, indicating maneuver areas required to avoid the protruding terrain.

Expanded displays.

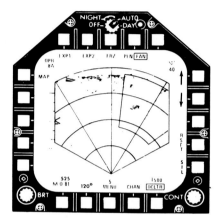

MAP VIDEO WITH SUPERIMPOSED EXP 1 FIELD OF VIEW INDICATOR

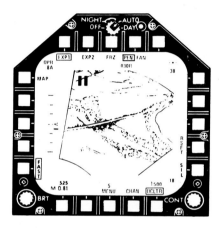

EXP 1 DISPLAY

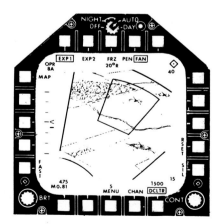

EXP 1 VIDEO WITH SUPERIMPOSED EXP 2 FIELD OF VIEW INDICATOR

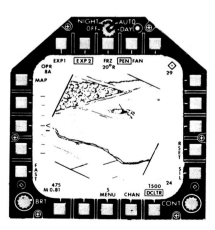

EXP 2 DISPLAY

Incredible photo of a CF-18 on a practice weapon delivery pass at the Jimmy Lake bombing range near Cold Lake. (S. Pshebylo)

Sunny '85

INTO SERVICE

The CF-18 implementation plan calls for garrison operations at Cold Lake, Alberta, Bagotville, Quebec and Baden-Soellingen in West Germany. Additional deployments are planned from bases on both coasts, such as Comox and Goose Bay. The operational concept ultimately foresees a role for the Hornet at five forward locations in Canada's far north, including Inuvik, Yellowknife, Iqaluit and Rankin Inlet in the Northwest Territories, as well as Kuujjuaq, Quebec.

Although the Hornet is an excellent aircraft, unexpected vertical tail surface fatigue weakening (since rectified), coupled with unusually harsh flying weather during the winter of 1984/1985 and a temporary shortage of spare parts, required some creative readjustment of the overall implementation schedule. A result was the move of 409 TFS from Cold Lake to Baden, and a delay in activating the NORAD West squadron. However, when Course Four graduated in the summer of 1986, the European transition process from the ageing CF-104 to CF-18 was completed; all three fighter squadrons forming 1 Canadian Air Group are now equipped with the Hornet. Beyond the crewing of new CF-18 units, two training courses are dedicated to existing squadron top-ups, graduating in December 1986 and June 1988. The entire process will conclude with the creation of all eight squadrons by the end of 1988. In keeping with the declared multi-role capability of this versatile aircraft, even NORAD squadrons with aircrew dedicated to the air superiority role will be required to weapons qualify to at least minimum NATO ground attack standards.

This Jim Baxter cartoon inspired by the CF-104 close-out in March 1986 succinctly captures the mood of the occasion. Although 1 CAG fighter pilots were sad to lose their trusty '104s, the Hornet has proven to be a worthy and popular successor to the Starfighter.

CF-18 operating locations

Yellowknife · Rankin Inlet · Iqaluit · Kuujjuaq · Goose Bay · Cold Lake · Comox · Bagotville

also
Baden-Soellingen, FRG ·

CF-18 Hornet Squadrons

Sqn.	Base	Aircraft	Role	Activation	Name
410 OTS	Cold Lake	23	training	June 1982	Cougar
425 TFS	Bagotville	12	Air Defence/ Surface Attack	April 1985	Alouette
409 TFS	Baden-Soellingen	16	Surface Attack/ Air Defence	June 1985	Nighthawk
439 TFS	Baden-Soellingen	16	Surface Attack/ Air Defence	December 1985	Tiger
421 TFS	Baden-Soellingen	16	Surface Attack/ Air Defence	June 1986	Red Indian
441 TFS	Cold Lake	12	Air Defence/ Surface Attack	July 1987	Silver Fox
433 TFS	Bagotville	12	Surface Attack/ Air Defence	December 1987	Porcupine
416 TFS	Cold Lake	12	Surface Attack/ Air Defence	December 1988	Lynx

Notes
After receiving its first CF-18s in autumn 1982, 410 Sqn. spent the following year checking-out an initial cadre of instructor pilots to flush out its own training resources. The Cougars officially went into business as the Hornet Operational Training Squadron in January 1984 and are also tasked to augment other operational units as required. 409 Sqn. was formed at Cold Lake in August 1984.

LEARNING THE AIRCRAFT

The ardent desire of every aspiring Canadian Forces fighter pilot is one day to become fully accredited on the CF-18. 410 OTS at Cold Lake uses a combination of art and science to achieve this goal. The course is a long and demanding six months, and requires as a prerequisite either the extensive fighter pilot lead-in conversion course on CF-5s, or other tactical fighter pilot experience.

Beginning in "the schoolhouse," a healthy and often repeated dose of groundschool is dispensed. However, new teaching techniques have been introduced to match the high technology of the aircraft. Computer assisted instruction and teaching aids are used extensively to impart required systems information, with the added benefit of allowing CF-18 students to work at their own pace. Anyone unfamiliar with comput-

ers can safely learn their idiosyncrasies in class before tackling more sophisticated hardware on the flight line. Only a few conventional lectures are given by the instructional staff to test progress and cover material that requires a more personal touch.

As can be seen from the rather formidable-looking syllabus, the CF-18 is a very complex weapons system, and a considerable amount of school time is logged before the budding CF-18 pilot even *sees* a Hornet up close, let alone is allowed to touch one.

Nevertheless, groundschool academics are only one of a trio of teaching aids, the others being mechanical simulators and the Hornet itself. There are two simulator types. HOTAS cockpit trainers are partial task trainers used for performing cockpit drills and checks and for practicing emergencies. They are also used later to teach switchology and the required button-pushing sequences in the more tactically oriented phases of the course. "Big brother" to the HOTAS trainers is a full mission, single-dome Weapons

System Trainer (WST), used extensively during initial conversion and Airborne Intercept (AI) training, as well as for realistically practicing Air-to-Ground delivery switchology.

About the time the CF-18 student is beginning to despair of ever getting down to the flight line, the initial preparation for flying is complete and it's time to go. Academic and simulator time will continue to be interwoven around flying for the remainder of the course. Flying instruction is for the most part grouped in phases. Within phases and within the course, the flying syllabus is structured on the "building block" principle; making each mission more difficult and challenging as individual expertise grows. Flying training culminates with highly

Winter start at 410 Sqn., March 1983. Night formation strip reference lights are standard on the fin, aft fuselage and nose of all CF-18s for precise station-keeping. They are visually arranged in various unique patterns depending on aircraft formation position.

CF-18 Academic instruction	
Subject	Hourly Periods
Aircraft Operating Instructions	23
Safety Equipment	2
Communications/Navigation Systems	9
APG-65 radar	14
Mission Planning	6
Air-to-Air Weapons	10
CF-18 Air-to-Air Fire Control System	4
Intercept Tactics and Techniques	12
Aerial Attack Tactics	15
Air-to-Air Mission Planning	4
Conventional Air-to-Surface Weapons	8
CF-18 Air-to-Surface Fire Control System	8
Air-to-Surface Tactics	10
Electronic Warfare	15
NATO/NORAD Operations	25
TAC EVAL scenario	10
Total Academics	175
Examination and Review	24
Student Administration	4
Total	203

demanding Air-to-Surface tactics, replicating real conflict scenarios and bringing together the requirements for proficiency in all phases of tactical flying, including navigation, weapons delivery and aerial combat. Six months after walking through the front door, our fledgling has made the grade, but the learning process is far from complete. The Cougars train pilots to Limited Combat Ready (LCR) status, which will permit subsequent upgrading to Combat Ready and follow-on leader status on an operational CF-18 squadron.

Air Instruction	Trip			Hours		
	Dual	Solo	Total	Dual	Solo	Total
Clear Hood Transition	3	1	4	3.6	1.2	4.8
Instrument Transition	4	-	4	5.7	-	5.7
Formation Transition	2	1	3	2.6	1.2	3.8
Night Transition	1	1	2	1.5	1.5	3.0
Visual Navigation	1	1	2	1.2	1.2	2.4
Radar Navigation	1	-	1	1.3	-	1.3
Air Intercept	6	3	9	9.1	4.7	13.8
Basic Fighter Maneuvers	3	2	5	2.4	1.8	4.2
Air Combat Maneuvers	5	6	11	4.6	6.1	10.7
Air-to-Air Gunnery	1	-	1	1.0	-	1.0
Conventional Weapons Delivery	3	4	7	3.0	4.4	7.4
Air-to-Surface Tactics	5	4	9	5.6	4.8	10.4
Total Air Instruction CF-18	35	23	58	41.6	26.9	68.5

Simulator Instruction	
Subject	Hourly *Periods*
Cockpit Familiarization	1
Start/Shut Down Procedures	2
Emergencies	1
Comm/Nav Procedures	2
A/A Switchology	1
A/G Switchology	1
BFM/ACM Procedures	1
Air-to-Surface Procedures	1
Total HOTAS	10

Subject	*Periods*	*Hours*
Handling and Emergencies	3	3
IFR Practice and Emergencies	4	4
Air Intercept	9	9
Basic Fighter Maneuvers	4	2
Air Combat Maneuvering	5	3
Air-to-Air Gunnery	1	1
Conventional Air-to-Surface Weapons	4	4
Electronic Warfare	3	3
Total WST	33	29
Briefings and Debriefings		33

A graduation certificate is merely a licence to learn; and that learning is a neverending process throughout the Hornet pilot's entire operational life.

Hornet cockpit illuminated for night flying. Right DDI features a radar display; centre HI, navigational information; and left DDI, stores management data. (McDonnell Douglas)

FLIGHT PROFILE

Initial impressions on the pre-flight CF-18 walkaround are of the aircraft's great size and its extreme strength and robustness, from the complex main undercarriage members to the sheer enormity of the fuselage and wings. With missiles, wingspan is over 40 feet; from tarmac to vertical fin tops, more than 15 feet.

Strapping-in is a treat to the senses, which are inundated by the array of new technology in the cockpit, not to mention that unique "new car smell." (Yes, it's true. The combination of machined metal, fabrics, plastics, electronic components and fresh paint can combine to give airplanes the same aroma.) Next, the eyes register some very distinct differences over earlier generation aircraft; cockpit instrumentation looks like something from *Star Wars*. About the only conventional-looking instruments visible are an altimeter, airspeed indicator, vertical speed indicator and a small artificial horizon just over the pilot's right knee. These are strictly standby instruments, powered through an inverter from the aircraft's batteries in the event of a complete AC power failure. The cockpit is dominated by three DDIs and the Up Front Controller squarely centred between them. In fact, even the conventional "round dials" or vertical tapes for the engines are missing, their place being taken by an engine monitor display panel, or a more elaborate presentation that may be called up on the DDIs. In both cases, presentations are strictly digital and take some time to become familiar with, since they lack the stability of the more conventional dial. This type of system is very much in keeping with a new presentation philosophy. As opposed

to a rising, falling or flickering needle on a dial, the pilot is alerted to impending trouble by warning lights, and a marvel known as "Betty the Bitch." "Betty" is the CF-18's innovative voice alert system; an unfailingly correct (though rather monotonous) female voice which advises of all aircraft system faults, degradations and emergency or cautionary situations requiring action by the pilot. "Betty" has acquired her nickname not due to her sex, but rather to her nagging nature.

Start-up drills are very straightforward and logical although the post-start period gets a trifle busy due to the requirement for a host of BIT checks as well as systems programming. These involve a great deal of "button pushing" as the various systems are made ready for flight. Programming and checking the various computers is in fact one of the more complex pilot chores; actual flight is relatively straightforward.

Strapped-in with the canopy closed, one has the sensation of sitting *on* rather than *in* the aircraft, due to excellent visibility from the large, unrestricted canopy and

the low canopy frame itself. Innovative features continue to appear, including dual mode nosewheel steering; of which one is similar to most aircraft. However, the high steering mode allows the aircraft to turn just about sideways and disappear up its own tailpipes — very handy for safe, efficient maneuvering in congested areas.

Takeoff is routine, and, unlike the CF-104 and CF-5, there is so much excess thrust available that afterburner power is normally not selected. When an afterburner takeoff is performed it is always a memorable event, a real eye-opener guaranteed to roll anybody's socks down. Acceleration is very smooth and tremendously rapid; care must be exercised not to overspeed the landing gear on retraction or to accidently go supersonic during climbout. The aircraft accelerates quite quickly even in Military Power (full power without afterburner) and initially the tendency is to "get behind," anticipation being the key here. During takeoff roll, the

Afterburner takeoff at Cold Lake. The aircraft is still within the airfield boundary at this point. August 6, 1985.

stick should be held neutral and directional control is maintained using nose wheel steering, not differential brakes. At the calculated nose wheel liftoff speed, smooth aft stick pressure is applied to raise the small "W" or aircraft waterline symbol on the HUD to 7° nose up. This attitude is held until the aircraft unsticks, which is quickly, even in MIL. Safely airborne with landing gear and flaps selected up, the waterline symbol disappears, and the velocity vector symbol (indicating where the aircraft is going), now becomes the main aircraft reference. This is kept at 2-3° nose up on the pitch ladder while accelerating to 325 knots. At 325 knots, the velocity vector is rotated to 10-15° nose up, then 350 knots is maintained until reaching Mach .85 or cruise Mach. The spacious cockpit has been designed for optimum lookout, and with all flight data

displayed the HUD becomes very familiar in no time at all; a real advantage to the fighter pilot, whose primary attention lies in events happening *outside* the cockpit.

Another technological advancement is an automatic trim function in pitch when the flaps and landing gear are up. This feature is a bit disconcerting at first, tending to remove one of the pilot's time-honoured "seat of the pants" cues for aircraft acceleration and deceleration. However, it has proven to be a valuable tool and an improvement over conventional trim mechanisms.

Only when airborne and in the process of maneuvering do the Hornet's exceptional performance characteristics become apparent. Basic handling qualities are so docile that it has prompted the expression, "Your granny can fly it..." The work comes in learning to maximize the CF-18's

tremendous potential, both aerodynamically and through its many sophisticated systems. Whereas acres of airspace were needed to turn a CF-104 in air combat, the close-in hard-turning characteristics of the Hornet have been likened to "a knife fight in a telephone booth." The airplane just naturally prompts superlatives, such as "a Ten," "a Buck Rogers fighter," and "the perfect aircraft for the times we're in."

In maneuvering flight aircraft AOIs say, "there is a light but constant stick force per g (about 3.5 to 4.5 pounds/g). Unlike many other airplanes, maneuvering stick forces do not vary significantly over the entire operating envelope so long as Angle of Attack (AOA) is less than the feedback AOA of 22°." The "book" tells the pilot to use caution during low speed overhead maneuvers as the airplane tends to enter a tailslide. Aft stick must be increased near

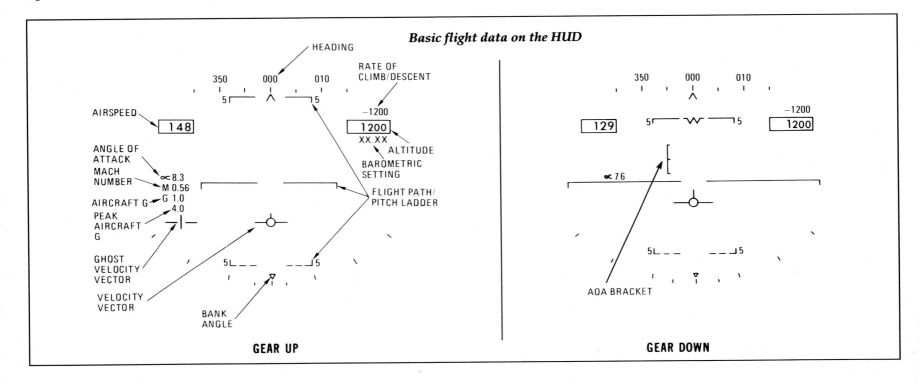

Basic flight data on the HUD

GEAR UP

GEAR DOWN

the top of a slow speed loop to maintain a positive pitch rate, and should be held until the nose is below the horizon and the airspeed is increasing. Inertial pitch coupling occurs when rolling at an AOA above 20°, and typical maneuvers that cause this type of coupling are high-g barrel and rudder rolls beyond limits. Aggressive maneuvering and use of rudder is just fine in the Hornet, as long as the yaw rate is actively controlled during these maneuvers to avoid pitch coupling. To assist the pilot, designers have thoughtfully provided yet another innovation; a beeping tone that warns of a yaw rate over 25°/second, which is to be avoided. The CF-18 has a good roll rate throughout the entire flight envelope but at higher AOA (over 30°) directional response and AOA cannot be controlled precisely. From 35-40° AOA, longitudinal and lateral directional stability decreases. "In this region, rudder power is adequate for maintaining essentially wings level flight but large sideslip excursions can occur. Sideslip excursions in the region are further aggravated with the centreline tank loaded. Longitudinal response above 37° AOA is very good; however, precise AOA control is not possible. Full aft stick results in maximum AOAs between 55° and 60°. At full aft stick in a stall, the airplane is stable with small pitch and roll oscillations, large nondivergent sideslip oscillations, and a high rate of descent (18,000 fpm). Loud airframe vortex rumbling noises are heard in the cockpit in the 55° to 60° AOA region. At Mach numbers greater than 0.8 at AOA greater than 20°, roll control is significantly reduced to prevent nose slice departures."

So the Hornet, like any aircraft, has limits. However, they're very broad and leave a great deal of room to "get the job done." A few basic maneuvering examples will illustrate what pulling the Hornet around is like... A Split S is begun 20,000 feet above ground (AGL) and 200 knots. The pilot then rolls inverted, advances the throttles to MIL and pulls up to 25° AOA, maintains this AOA until 4g is reached and holds 4g until recovery to level flight is made 180° off the entry heading. A maximum rate Split S can be performed as already described but with full aft stick to 30-35° AOA. If afterburners are selected going through the vertical, this maneuver can be completed in only 3,000-4,000 feet with no loss in airspeed. To perform a Vertical Eight, after attaining entry parameters of 8,000-10,000 feet AGL and 500 knots, the pilot selects afterburner and commences a 5g pull into the vertical.

Single and dual 410 Sqn. Hornets over the 12,000 foot Cold Lake inner runway. There is a considerable size difference between the two cockpit canopies.

While doing this, the anti-g suit valve meters vital engine bleed air to rubber bladders strapped to the pilot's legs and midriff, which then inflate and increase tolerance to blackout by reducing blood drain from the brain during tight turns. There is no problem maintaining 5g until the CF-18 is inverted. At this point, with airspeed around 300 knots, the pilot rolls the aircraft upright and performs a slow loop, that is, 4g until 25° AOA. On completion of this loop, afterburners are deselected and an inverted roll is initiated to complete the lower half of the circle in idle power at 5gs or 25° AOA. Proper execution of this maneuver results in an altitude gain of about 5,000 feet. Exhilarating, and it doesn't take much imagination to think of practical applications for these performance capabilities, like carving down on some unsuspecting adversary in a sweeping, scythe-like turn...

Sooner or later, the laws of physics prevail and what goes up must come down. If an instrument approach is required, there are very few instrument certified airports that can't be used, as a pilot has the INS and radar, and also ADF, VOR, TACAN and ILS to choose from.

A TACAN penetration is flown at 280 knots and 80% RPM with speed brakes out and flaps in AUTO mode. About 8°-10° nose down pitch is needed to sustain 280 knots under these conditions. After levelling off, airspeed is reduced to 230-250 knots, speed brakes selected in, and at two

Superb visibility is evident in this rear seat view from a dual. The aircraft is being flown slightly offset in line astern formation on the leader.
A visitor to CFB Cold Lake gets the complete sensation of Hornet flying at its best, courtesy the Cougars. The helmet style is not regular issue for squadron pilots. (Nick Lees photos)

Jet penetration/TACAN approach

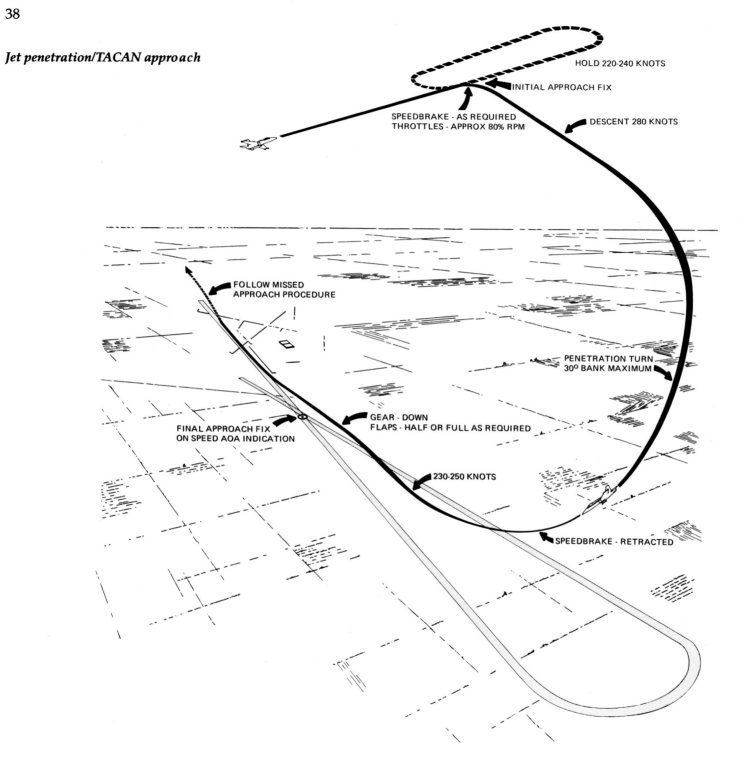

HOLD 220-240 KNOTS

INITIAL APPROACH FIX

SPEEDBRAKE - AS REQUIRED
THROTTLES - APPROX 80% RPM

DESCENT 280 KNOTS

FOLLOW MISSED
APPROACH PROCEDURE

PENETRATION TURN
30° BANK MAXIMUM

GEAR - DOWN
FLAPS - HALF OR FULL AS REQUIRED

FINAL APPROACH FIX
ON SPEED AOA INDICATION

230-250 KNOTS

SPEEDBRAKE - RETRACTED

miles prior to the final descent point, landing gear is selected down and flaps to FULL. Just prior to descent, the Hornet pilot keeps the velocity vector on the horizon line and when at the Final Approach Fix, he simply reduces the throttles 1-2%, lowers the velocity vector 3° (700 fpm rate of descent) and maintains the on-speed AOA with power. This on-speed AOA consists of superimposing the AOA bracket (or "E" Bracket, as it is more often called) on the left side of the velocity vector and keeping it there. As the AUTO

Looking like a case history from an aerodynamics textbook, a transonic shock wave of tortured water vapour is superimposed on this fast moving, hard maneuvering Hornet.

trim function is now disengaged, aft pitch trim will be required, and since the power response is very sensitive in the CF-18, only small corrections are necessary. Average fuel burn during a high level letdown is about 700 pounds but can be a miserly 300 if an idle descent profile is used.

All that remains after a successful approach is to get the machine on the ground. To use a standard example, the CF-18 pilot has now arrived at a position around 300-400 feet AGL one mile from the runway and is "on speed" for landing, approximately 120 knots plus 3 knots for every 1,000 pounds of fuel remaining. Designed as a carrier aircraft, the Hornet must land at a higher than normal rate of descent, but in an exact spot. The aircraft is not flared but instead flown onto the runway in its final approach attitude, seemingly with little finesse in a "controlled crash." An abrupt arrival is necessary to fully compress the landing gear and close a "weight-on-wheels" microswitch. Normal braking, nose wheel steering, and a reduction of throttles to ground idle is then possible. This type of landing has several benefits such as reduced landing roll and brake wear. Touchdown spot can be controlled precisely, a tremendous advantage at short fields or in approach-end barrier engagements. For the "perfect" Hornet landing, the pilot places the HUD velocity vector at the beginning of the touchdown marker bars painted on the runway. The "E" bracket is now captured and accurately maintained with pitch, power being used to control rate of descent. The velocity vector also provides the pilot with the aircraft's actual glide path; if this is 2.5° nose low from the horizon, all is well for an ideal approach. Accurate adjustments to the glide path can easily be accomplished.

Crabbing is allowed while on final and the correct crosswind technique for landing is to remove half the crab prior to touchdown by applying an appropriate amount of rudder and keeping the wings level with aileron.

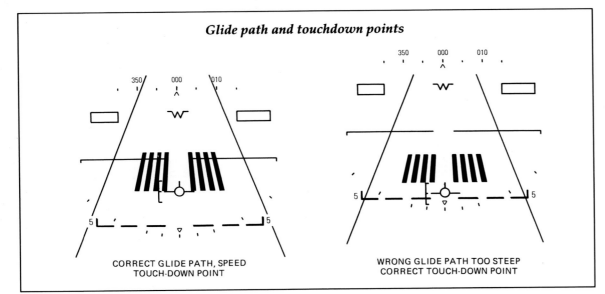

Glide path and touchdown points

CORRECT GLIDE PATH, SPEED
TOUCH-DOWN POINT

WRONG GLIDE PATH TOO STEEP
CORRECT TOUCH-DOWN POINT

SQUADRON COLOURS

*Tail markings of the European-based CF-18
squadrons. Left to right: 409, 421, and 439 Sqn.*

425 (Alouette) Squadron CF-18A Hornet based at Bagotville, Quebec, November 1986. This aircraft is fitted with live missiles.

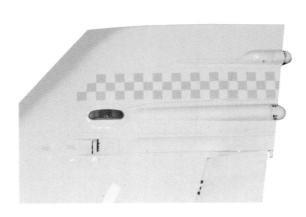

The famous checkerboard insignia of 441 Sqn. marks the arrival of the Hornet's newest converts.

PUTTING IT ALL TOGETHER

"Mako Three right."

"Mako Four."

"Mako Lead, Mako Three and Four approaching south point, angels two-five."

"Roger Mako Three, Mako Lead and Two are anchor north point. You're cleared frequency."

"Rog. Mako Four go channel one-five left."

In two separate CF-18 cockpits, gloved hands reach forward to the Up Front Controller to change radio frequencies from the right radio to the left radio and to the GCI controller, who eagerly awaits their arrival.

The place is the Cold Lake air combat maneuvering range in the dead of winter. The situation: Two-versus-Two intercepts with visiting F-106 interceptors from the USAF Air National Guard. The Americans are up to exercise by invitation and are trained in Warsaw Pact adversary tactics. As their aircraft bear a close resemblance to earlier series MiGs, they represent excellent training value as flying threat simulators.

"Mako Three left."

"Mako Four."

"Gladstone Control, Mako Three and Four up for your control."

"Roger Mako Three, you have 50 miles separation, anchor south and climb angels two-nine. Call ready."

Quickly, the two CF-18s spiral up to 29,000 feet and complete the last of their pre-engagement cockpit checks, including fuel, weapons, radar, essential switchology and video recording camera — that vital "argument-settler" for the fighter pilot.

"Mako Three and Four level angels two-niner. Three ready with nine point two. VTR on."

"Mako Four ready with nine point zero. VTR on."

"Roger Three and Four, the fight's on. Come left 360°. Target's 360° for 54 miles."

"Roger, 360°. Four go spread."

"Four."

Like two of the grey aquatic predators whose name they carry, Mako Three and Four cruise north out of their holding point, accelerating to 500 knots in a line-abreast spread formation, with about 5,000 feet of lateral separation. They are sleek, menacing and deliberately looking for trouble...

Today the F-106s, who took off first, have been given the task of simulating a Canadian airspace penetration with hostile intent. It is Mako Three and Four's job to stop them.

Although the CF-18 possesses classified equipment to identify an "unknown" in weather or beyond visual range (BVR), and the appropriate radar-guided AIM-7 Sparrow ordnance, that capability is not part of today's scenario. Nor will GCI radar confirm that the bogeys are indeed bandits (hostile). Instead, the Hornets are simulating the requirement to perform a tactical visual identification or VID, prior to shooting. In this exercise our fighter pilots are limited to an engagement and ordnance that effectively ties one hand behind their backs; *visual* employment of both missiles and cannon. "FOX ONEs," or simulated BVR Sparrow shots will be taken today if the shot parameters are acquired. However, it will be just for the shooter's practice, have no bearing on the engagement, and will not be honoured by the traditional sock-rolling high-g missile break turn by the opponent.

The Makos streak north in their classic Double Attack formation optimized for mutual support and lookout. In both cockpits, sure hands busy themselves on the HOTAS controls in the practiced routine of predetermined tasks. It's called "playing the piccolo" in any HOTAS-engineered fighter; a phrase which aptly describes the flurry of constant activity over throttle and stick, which carry a myriad of multi-function buttons and switches. One of the beauties of this system is that once the HOTAS skills are mastered, just about everything needed to make the "kill" is literally at one's fingertips.

Compared to the raw violence of straining turbofans scant feet from the pilot, the cockpit is almost serenely quiet. Only a muted hum from the air conditioning and pressurization system, and the pilot's rhythmic breathing in his oxygen mask, can be heard over a faint background radio hiss.

The Double Attack pair are busy with pre-briefed responsibilities. Mako Three as element leader uses his radar to search the vast airspace below to level with his horizon. Mako Four, the designated wingman, searches above, and down to the horizon. Although the two opposing pairs of fighters start with over 50 miles of separation, due to closing velocities there is only about two and a half minutes between them at best, and so *much* to accomplish in that short time. Suddenly, it happens... The side-to-side sweep of the radar cursors is starting to bring results...

"Mako Three contact, 350°, thirty-six miles, angels two six."

"Mako Four, same."

Initial contact with the unknowns has now occurred. They must be isolated to one side of the formation and their future actions made as predictable as possible. Since the aerial geometry of the engagement dictates a right-to-left pass with Three and Four passing right, Mako Four flies to the right of Three, looking into the threat. Three will primarily be the "eyeball," designated to make a VID on the bogies; Four will be concerned with positioning himself for a quick "kill" on at least one of the bogies. This does *not*, however, preclude *both* fighters from locking-up and shooting at separate targets if the opportunity presents itself. On the attack, the eyeball is attempting to arrive several miles in front of the bandits with a modest amount of target aspect. The shooter is maintaining close combat spread until some distance prior to this point; then he takes a split in heading. The sorting of "who is where" within the "enemy" formation should be complete shortly thereafter.

Why is this geometry so important? The threat is put to one side of the defending element's flight path, which makes keeping track of them easier; the element can remain close together longer, providing more mutual support; the element is brought through the area where the look

Capt. Sean Hanrahan enroute to some dissimilar air combat training with two 134th TFS F-16s from Burlington, Vermont flown by Capts. Phil Murdock and Doug Hiller. The F-16's aerodynamic properties closely approximate those of the MiG-29 Fulcrum. Spring, 1987. (P. Blais)

angle is optimized for RAID mode usage on the radar; the bogies are placed in an easier position to VID, since they show more aspect angle; and since the eyeball is going pure pursuit on his target, the shooter can project his partner's nose position to aid in his own "tallyho" of the enemy. Lastly, these tactics place the bogies in a reactive situation. If they continue on their present course, the attack parameters have been solved; if the bogies turn into the attack, they must shift formation and (more importantly) throw up a wing to make the turn, thus making VID easier.

Once the element has set this attack positioning, both eyeball and shooter should attempt to "sort" the close formation by using a combination of TWS, RWS and RAID modes. RAID is better left primarily to the shooter, as it requires some patience to resolve, and may not break out the formation until in to closer range. Meanwhile, the eyeball continues to monitor the "big picture" by using TWS to sanitize the area of other hostiles, then back in to RWS mode. Soon, the ever-decreasing range dictates that it's time for Single Target Track (STT). Having already armed for Sparrow by pushing the weapons select switch forward on the left side of the control stick, Mako Three quickly changes to STT mode and is greeted with the flashing SHOOT cues of a Sparrow solution on his HUD.

"FOX ONE, FOX ONE on the lead bandit heading south at twenty-six thousand."

Only the absence of a live missile today, and the lack of a final safeguarding step in the arming sequence, keep a Sparrow from torching off the CF-18's belly, and streaking its way across the rapidly narrowing gap of sky between friend and foe, with the full intention of performing a frontal

lobotomy on that lead bandit.

"Roger, continue."

The Sparrow shot was called because the pilot achieved the previously mentioned shot parameters, but with the rules of the day, it's not a "kill" and the fight is still on.

About this time, Four, who along with Three has been experimenting with RAID mode, makes a welcome call.

"Mako Four has a sort. They're stacked left. Mako Four is locked-on trailer."

In both cockpits, eager thumbs have flicked the weapons select switch down to the Sidewinder position and the heat-seeking missile heads slave themselves to the aircraft's radar.

"Rog, Three's locked-on the lead."

Now the excitement level is intense. A rectangular hollow green box on the HUD narrows the field of view required for the two CF-18 pilots to find the bogies. *Somewhere* inside that box....

Starting a pure pursuit curve at the targets inside ten miles, pulses rapidly increase as range closes fast and time starts

Two Cougars on the prowl, 1983. False canopy belly markings were designed to produce momentary hesitation on the part of an adversary by creating confusion as to the direction of turn. They are unique to Canadian Hornets.

to run out. Then, a big, grey delta wing flashes in planform within the green box on the HUD...

"BANDITS, BANDITS, BANDITS... Mako Four, cleared to fire."

Right index fingers in two separate Hornet cockpits close tightly on stick grip triggers, and the two Makos are quickly exiting the engagement area to the north, past the simulated fireballs of their intended victims. Mako Three pulls back the throttles to conserve precious fuel, while calling "Knock it off, knock it off" on the radio. Time to set up for another attack scenario. Because the intercept was a complete success there was no need to exercise any one of a host of options required had they missed back there at the merge. No close-in maneuvering was necessary. The next time, who knows?

Gear down, flaps down, hook down... a Hornet comes out of the dusk on a short final approach for an arrested landing.

EUROPEAN OPERATIONS

Idyllically located on the Rhine near Baden-Baden, CFB Baden-Soellingen is tucked into a picturesque valley between the Black Forest Hills or Schwartzwald in Germany, and the Vosges mountains of Alsace-Lorraine in France. The trick for the average CF-18 pilot in 1 CAG is finding the time to enjoy the marvellous ambiance of the area. Compared with work routines in the CF-104 era, the Hornet's increased capability and multiplicity of roles has led one squadron commander to comment, "Nothing to it really. We just come in, work your average twelve hour day, then go home again..."

A fighter pilot's day in central Europe begins early, typically with a mass squadron weather or "met" briefing around 0700-0730, depending on when aircraft are scheduled to be airborne on their first missions. The met brief has traditionally been considered nearly a morning parade, as it's about the only occasion on which senior supervisors can be guaranteed a near-perfect attendance. Not only do the pilots receive a very detailed (and occasionally accurate!) forecast of weather throughout the flying area, but those present will be bombarded with administrative announcements, a detailed review of an aircraft system's "emergency of the day" and, always, some germane briefing such as an intelligence update on latest developments "the other side of the tracks." There may also be a recognition quiz on the adversary's equipment (land, air and even sea), or on increasingly complex and comprehensive battle procedures and plans. *All this* with the first cup of coffee. His day may have started even earlier, depending on flight planning requirements or whether an early morning simulator mission has been scheduled.

After the communal briefings comes mission planning. Although the Europeans are very air-minded and enthusiastic in their support for NATO training needs, the sheer population density poses very different mission planning problems from those encountered in sparsely populated Canada. Restricted areas abound. Although everybody knows the shortest distance between two points is a straight line, the CF-18 pilot will rarely have an opportunity to fly it. Permanent restrictions are everywhere, such as airport control zones and large population centres. Add the chameleon-like nature of the *temporary* restriction board covered with other forbidden zones including paradrop areas, glider activities or localized exercises, and the need to spend sufficient time on route and mission attack planning becomes obvious.

CF-18A seen taxiing out of its individual hardened aircraft shelter. Directly beneath the leading edge of the wing strake is the 600,000 candlepower quartz-halogen night-time visual identification light, another Canada-specific modification. Baden, summer 1986.

439 Sqn. aircraft. Cordite stains from the 20mm cannon mark the noses of these aircraft.

Since valuable flight time must be exploited to obtain the most training benefit, simulated attacks on several different targets are typical, each involving a great deal of forethought and preparation. Most air-to-ground tactical missions involve at least a two-target scenario, then a role change into low level CAP with or without GCI radar or AWACS. Many planning variables must be considered, including the target's suitability to attack from the number of aircraft available.

One very fickle variable is weather. The novice fighter pilot quickly learns to plan for every possible weather contingency, including how and where he will abort at any given stage of his route *without* violating some sacrosanct airspace. CF-18 pilots

also share European airspace with the nations of two Allied Tactical Air Forces (ATAFs) and a large French tactical air force. Weather can be regionally changeable, and often there is only one suitable flying area on the whole continent, such as southern Bavaria or the North German Plain. Traffic flow problems within these suddenly highly congested blocks of airspace require extreme vigilance, both in planning and mission execution. Built-in electronic sensors are no substitute for an alert pair of eyes, and fighter pilots quickly

Two CF-18s make a formation low approach. These aircraft are in the ferry configuration, each carrying three 330 US gallon external fuel tanks.

learn to appreciate that disciplined lookout and visual search patterns are absolutely essential to survival. Squadron turtleneck sweaters keep the pilot's neck from being rubbed raw by harness straps and life support equipment, given the near-constant head turning as the skies are scanned for a tell-tale smoke plume, a flash of reflected light on metal, or relative motion against a stationary background, warning of other aircraft near his flight path.

With the CF-18 there are far fewer bad weather "no fly" days. Capt. Tom Sweeney, who also flew the CF-104 in Europe explains: "If no air-to-ground areas are open, we swing up to the TRA for air combat (a temporary restricted airspace directly overhead Baden-Soellingen). If cloud tops are high, we go *very* high and do intercepts." When the weather really *is* bad, the omnipresent

WO Vic Johnson on a photo mission over Germany, 1986.
"High performance aviation photography poses numerous problems directly related to the task. These include heavy g loads, rapid pressure changes, disorientation and sometimes violent maneuvers. Additional discomfort is caused by the usual paraphernalia associated with fighter aircraft — straps, cords, hoses, wires, helmet and mask.

The 3.2 kilogram or 7.1 lb. Hasselblad EL electric drive camera is used almost exclusively and gives me the quality and image size essential for display enlargements. Under 5g conditions the camera suddenly weighs 16 kilos or 35 pounds. Also multiply my arm weight by five and the challenge "to get the shot" becomes apparent!

Good advance planning and an effective g suit makes a difficult situation much easier. Excellent all-around visibility, almost unlimited power, maneuverability and a great range of speeds, makes the Hornet a photographer's dream platform."

Squadron Operations Officer will undoubtedly schedule an extra large dosage of groundschool, much to the chagrin of earthbound pilots. And so, a more mundane but vital aspect of life in a NATO fighter squadron continues, unfortunately without the wonderful release of flight...

Weather permitting, scheduled missions include dissimilar air combat training with any number of eager adversaries from other air forces, individual low-level navigation missions, formation tactics against simulated targets around the countryside, or the deployment of a formation to conventional weapons ranges at Siegenberg, Pampa or Suippes in Germany, Belgium and France respectively, in order to hone bombing, rocketry and gunnery skills. The latter are always flown in some type of battle formation to enhance lookout and practice transiting and turning in collective situations.

Some range events may be limited to rectangular overhead patterns, highly

Proof that one picture really can be worth a 1,000 words is amply demonstrated by this exceptional photo which captures the thrill of operational flying, if only for a brief moment.

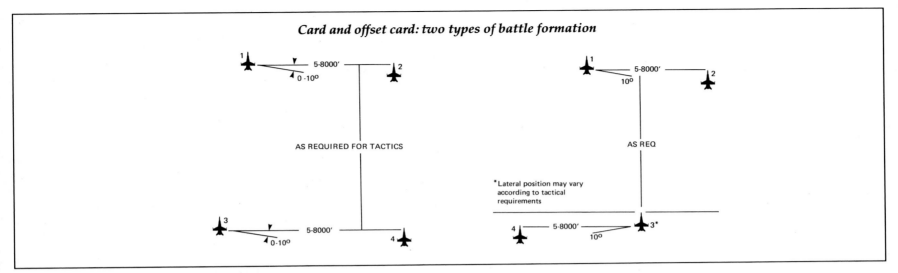

Card and offset card: two types of battle formation

predictable as all aircraft attack in sequence on the same heading, at a regular interval, and are completely visible and exposed throughout the pattern. However, CF-18 pilots prefer to spend much of their time on tactically viable deliveries — low-level, high-speed run-ins, an abrupt pull-up short of the target, followed by a rapid, diving roll-in and last minute change of direction to put ordnance on target. Such tactics are practised at various airspeed combinations and dive angles with bombs, rockets and the cannon, reducing exposure time to enemy retaliation from below. Deliveries are planned for prevailing weather conditions, ordnance type carried, target type selected and target terrain conditions. Variations on this theme of "unpredictability" are also available for level bombing, consisting of a high-speed level run-in tangential to the target, a high g curvilinear turn

Two 439 Sqn. Hornets in a formation takeoff from Kleine Brogel, Belgium, during the multinational Tactical Air Meet '86.

towards the target, and, in the last seconds, a wings-level rollout just in time to release the weapons.

A typical range mission could easily entail several passes of different events, for example, 5° high drag bombs, 15° rockets and perhaps 20° tactical strafe followed by a rejoin to battle formation and departure from the range. To test the flight's situational awareness, a "Red Baron" or single adversary may have been designated to run an intercept and elicit a realistic response. This procedure tests lookout techniques, providing a forum for later evaluation of the all-important initial response to a hostile aircraft. Attacks on a tactical formation are structured and very much in keeping with pre-ordained Rules of Engagement.

Approaching home base, any formation members with "hung" ordnance will make a straight-in approach without overflying populated areas. As a tactically preferred recovery option, straight-in finals are now practised to avoid being shot down by friendly (and in wartime, understandably nervous) airfield defences.

However, given acceptable weather and conditions, the flight leader may choose the more venerable "battle break" recovery designed to reduce vulnerability by minimizing the time a formation spends over the airfield at circuit altitude and speed. It consists of a high-speed, low-level run in a spread "finger" formation to overfly the runway landing threshold followed by an abrupt, sequential pull-up to the downwind position in the circuit for normal individual stream landings. The spacing between aircraft is acquired by the timing and intensity of the pull-up. Fighter pilots practice this tactic for its wartime applications, and if it looks like too much *fun*, that's just a fringe benefit...

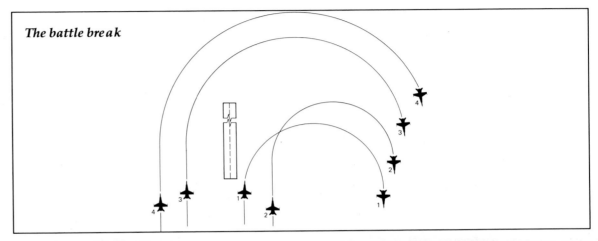

The battle break

Air weapons technicians Glen Miller and Ruth Tracey install a 20mm Vulcan cannon. The APG-65 radar antenna has been fitted with a red plastic protective cover and the air-to-air refuelling probe is extended.

The SUU-20 training weapons dispenser is capable of holding six practice bombs and four 2.75" rockets. Baden-Soellingen, 1986.

SAFETY RECORD

October 1987 marks five years of experience on the CF-18 for the Canadian Forces. As of this writing, four aircraft have been destroyed with pilot fatalities in two instances. (The most recent loss was in the Bagotville area during September 1987. Major Mike Stacey ejected and the accident is presently under investigation.) A fifth Hornet is extensively damaged, but may be repaired. In terms of actual flying hours, the low accident rate constitutes a superior performance and is actually below forecast attrition figures.

Accident Summary

On April 12, 1984, CF-18 '715, flown by a student pilot on his twelfth AI (air intercept) mission, was involved in a one-on-one training exercise. On the sixth and final intercept, both fighter and T-33 target aircraft were approaching head-on with approximately 35 miles separation. The T-33 target was at a low altitude (1,000 feet AGL) heading east. The CF-18 started its run at 19,000 feet flying in a westerly direction, obtained a successful radar lock-on, and proceeded to fly the pre-briefed attack/reattack profile. As he was positioning himself for reattack, the pilot maintained a lower than normal altitude requiring a steeper than normal descent. About the time the CF-18 should have been rolling out behind the target aircraft, the T-33 pilot observed a fireball of ground impact not far from his position. An initial investigation revealed all aircraft systems appear to have been operating normally and the CF-18 was in controlled flight prior to impact. To add credence to this, no radio transmissions were made by the pilot, nor was there any attempt to eject.

While this accident remains somewhat unresolved, procedural error is suspected rather than a specific fault with the aircraft. Flight training scenarios and air combat Rules of Engagement have since been extensively modified to preclude a repetition of this event.

On June 4, 1985, 409 Sqn. CF-18 '737 was the lead of five aircraft lined up for departure at Cold Lake. Lead and Two rolled in formation, but at lift-off speed, Lead was unable to rotate and takeoff was aborted at high speed. The hook was deployed well before the arresting cable but failed to engage. The aircraft continued off the runway end, the landing gear collapsed, external fuel tanks ruptured and the aircraft caught fire, travelling an additional 2,500 feet before coming to rest. A successful ejection was made by the pilot who landed safely nearby with only minor injuries. The accident resulted in severe damage due to the selection of an improper stabilator trim setting prior to takeoff and a subsequent high speed abort late in the takeoff roll.

On May 24, 1986, at Summerside PEI, '717 of 425 Sqn. was returning to home base at the close of Armed Forces Day activities. Departure weather was a 300 foot cloud base topped at 4,500 feet and flight visibility of six miles. The aircraft performed an afterburner takeoff and climbed steeply into cloud, less than a minute later crashing into shallow water 200 yards offshore in Malpeque Bay. Insufficient evidence exists to identify a specific cause, but there is no reason to suspect any systems failure.

May 4, 1987, aircraft '919, a 439 Sqn. dual, departed controlled flight on a functional air test trip after routine maintenance. Unable to recover, the pilots ejected safely at around 10,000' AGL. The aircraft

crashed near the village of Zimmern, approximately 12 miles south of Baden-Soellingen.

On the lighter side, CF-18 aircrew have been responsible on several occasions for saving aircraft under adverse conditions. During the summer of 1985 a USN exchange pilot with 410 Sqn. on an air combat sortie rolled into a 135° bank slice turn at approximately 425 knots. Lt. Jim Braun recalls what happened: "The next radio call I heard was from the ACMR Range Officer calling someone 'dead' (a simulated kill). Not clear as to who had been shot, I questioned the call. This distracted me from the work at hand. I was pulling 7.7g in about 1.5 seconds and unknown to me, my g-suit had also come unplugged prior to the engagement. Just as I was questioning who had been shot, I lost consciousness. There was absolutely no warning that this was about to occur. I have previously experienced 'greyout' and 'blackout', but never really expected that unconsciousness could occur to *me* so quickly."

Lt. Braun remembered coming to, seeing the inside of his eyelids and hearing his heart beating loudly as if it was between his ears. He felt very comfortable and relaxed, as if awakening from a sound sleep. Hearing a radio transmission from his wingman, vision returned and Braun found himself flying level at 12,000 ft. MSL, 480 knots. It was impossible to recall the exact flight situation immediately preceding blackout and he was still groggy. By making an issue out of this incident, Lt. Braun raised the awareness threshold of many pilots around him. The result is a vastly improved g-induced loss of consciousness awareness program including cautions on the use of the extremely effective aircraft g limiter, cautions against rapid onset g, improved straining maneuvers to help withstand blackout, and a rigorous physical training program designed to strengthen the upper body and improve g tolerance. Technical modifications are also forthcoming on the g suit valve, to meter air more rapidly to the suit under rapid g onset conditions.

Another incident involved Maj. Roy Mould flying a CF-18 as target for another during a Cold Lake intercept training mission. It was described in *Flight Comment*, the Canadian Forces flight safety magazine: "During a steep, high-speed descent to low level to negate the attacker, he experienced a violent nose-down pitch force of minus 3.7g. Recovery was effected by using both hands on the control column and by manually trimming the stabilator. By the time the aircraft was in controlled flight, it was noticed that the stabilators had reverted from the Control Augmentation System (CAS) mode to the Mechanical (MECH) mode and both Flight Control Computers had degraded. After climbing to a safe altitude, a reset of the flight controls was attempted. This resulted in another violent nose-down pitch movement from which a recovery to controlled flight was again made. Given the violent response of the aircraft to attempts to rectify the control problem, the pilot elected to leave the aircraft in MECH mode. The pilot assessed that he could control the aircraft by minimizing pitch and bank control column inputs, using trim for pitch control. With this technique, he did a controllability check and then set up for a long straight-in approach to a successful approach-end barrier engagement. This was the first time a CF-18 aircraft has been landed with the stabilators in MECH mode. (Maj. Mould) was commended for his accurate assessment of (a) difficult flight control emergency and for his professionalism in recovering a valuable aircraft."

Slightly the worse for wear, '737 rests forlornly among the approach lights at Cold Lake. The aircraft may be rebuilt.

HAPPENINGS

During the initial five years, specific events, opportunities and exercises have proven the Hornet's outstanding capabilities.

Heavyweight handling characteristics at low level are excellent. Excess power and superb flying qualities result in outstanding self-protection capabilities, even when cumbersome offensive weapons are retained. In short, the CF-18 has aerodynamic energy to spare, and highly effective flight controls.

Weapons delivery accuracies have exceeded all expectations. Using an example of one hundred and fifty 500 pound bombs dropped at 500 knots in a 20° dive, the average miss distances were three to four times better than those previously possible with the CF-104 and CF-5.

Close in, "go for the throat" air combat maneuvering capability against dissimilar aircraft is impressive. Performance against the F-15 and F-16 in all respects, including endurance with the F-15, shows the Hornet is *more* than capable of holding its own.

NORAD Intercepts

For some time the Soviet Union has been deploying military aircraft to the very fringes of Canadian airspace, in a perceived attempt to test our ability to respond. The Tupolev Tu-142 Bear-H carries the newest airborne radars, sensors and AS-15 Kent cruise missiles. While in the area the Russians conduct electronic reconnaissance and simulated cruise missile attacks. These aircraft, along with earlier Bear-D and Fs, regularly transit from Russia to Cuba entering the Canadian Air Defence Identification Zone (CADIZ) without a flight plan or prior notice, requiring rapid scrambling of interceptor aircraft for possible identification.

The appearance of the Bear-H with ALCM capability is cause for concern. An estimated cruise missile range of 3,000 kilometers places targets in southern Canada and the northern United States within striking range of these bombers, without any requirement even to enter North American airspace.

Canadian and US governments recently approved an air defence modernization program which will greatly improve

The essence of NORAD cooperation. 425 Sqn. CF-18s operating from CFS Gander and USAF 5th FIS F-15s of Minot, ND, launching out of Loring AFB, Maine, picked up this Bear-F Mod III in the early morning hours of April 28, 1987. Although the black and white photo is of low quality, it is the only available record showing the intercepting aircraft of both nations and the target together.

continental defensive capabilities. The North Warning System will include Over-the-Horizon Backscatter Radar and upgraded northern airfields.

Hornets are controlled and receive their intercept directions from the Canadian NORAD Region Operations Control Centre (ROCC) in North Bay. Routinely, two alert aircraft leave Bagotville late in the evening or early morning. At Gander they refuel and await an airborne order time from the North Bay controllers. From there a CAP is then established over the eastern Atlantic off Newfoundland. Soviet Bear aircraft usually travel in pairs at an altitude of just under 30,000 ft. Many intercepts take place during the dark hours, making photography difficult, but there have also been well-documented daylight encounters.

One of the early CF-18 "pipeliners," Capt. Frank Bergnach, graduated from the second course at Cold Lake before joining 425 Sqn. in April 1985. At 0200 hours on June 10, 1986, he was scrambled from Bagotville on a live intercept.

"After being up the greater part of the night, you should be tired, yet you're not. We don't normally practice intercepting aircraft that big and because our target is a propeller-driven airplane, up close you can hear the engines going and feel the vibration even in your own cockpit. The props are about 15 feet across and really kick up a lot of air. Exhilarating!"

The threat — Tupolev's big Bear-H, photographed by a CF-18 off Labrador, August 20, 1985. This variant lacks the distinctive rear fuselage observation blisters of its predecessors. The unusual vertical perspective provides a good idea of the comparative size of each aircraft.

While the intercept is underway the second CF-18 lies waiting several miles in trail, often rolling in later for a "photo opportunity." Close formation is maintained with the Bears and snapshots are duly exchanged between opposing crews for posterity.

Dawn patrol. Capt. Pete Van Langenhove pilots this 425 Sqn. machine. (Cam Witt)

Capt. Marcel Major on another Bagotville scramble. Live missiles are readily identified by their grey camouflage paint. Inert ordnance is coloured blue. November 3, 1986.

Exercise and Competition

The feasibility of operating CF-18s in the north was tested June 10-17, 1986, when four aircraft of 425 Sqn. conducted sustained flying operations from Frobisher Bay, NWT. Exercise Amalgam Chief '86 allowed the participants to practise and evaluate northern deployment under austere conditions, conduct air-to-surface tactical missions, aerial refuelling, and evaluate the control and communications network between NORAD and the CF-18 detachment at Frobisher Bay. The four Alouettes were logistically supported by

710 of 425 Sqn. takes on fuel over Baffin Island during Exercise Amalgam Chief 87-2. During the period of June 12-15, 410 and 425 Sqn. aircraft flew from Iqaluit, NWT, formerly Frobisher Bay.
How things look at the receiving end. The probe has engaged the "badminton bird" basket and fuel is now being taken on.

402 (Air Reserve) Sqn. flying the oldest Canadian Armed Forces fleet aircraft, the Douglas Dakota.

Combat Archer

To validate air-to-air missile stocks and evaluate the entire CF-18 missile system, including performance envelopes, a live firing missile program against remotely-piloted drones is conducted annually at the USAF Tyndall AFB missile test range in Florida.

Sophisticated electronic telemetry equipment mounted on the CF-18, the missiles and the target permits detailed analysis of all weapons system functions and the performance of the missile. In an effort to preserve targets, live warheads are deleted. Instead, the telemetry will record miss distance and arming functions to determine if the missile would have destroyed the target. Targets include very small MQM-107 drones and QF-100 Super

Sabre fighters, an aircraft retired from service and fitted with remote controls.

Although Canada has participated in similar evaluation programs with the CF-101 Voodoo, the October 1985 Combat Archer was the first opportunity to test the CF-18. A total of eight radar-guided AIM-7s and heat-seeking AIM-9s were fired by visiting 410 and 425 Sqn. aircraft using various target and fighter profiles designed and modified to prove and examine specific areas of missile employment. Under a Systems Effectiveness Monitoring Program (SEMP), *random* selections of missiles from operational stocks are fired as well.

The Florida trip provided an additional opportunity for combat training with F-16 Fighting Falcons, deployed to Tyndall, and F-15 Eagles from nearby Eglin AFB.

"Fox One". The launch of an AIM-7 radar guided missile. Exercise Combat Archer, 1985.

William Tell

Tyndall Air Force Base was also a scene of intense activity and drama in October 1986 as it hosted the prestigious biennial competition, William Tell '86. Sponsored by USAF Tactical Air Command, the meet is designed to test all phases of air defence in a realistic, live firing environment. Ten teams competed in two categories, F-15/CF-18 and F-4. The Canadians were down for the first time with the CF-18, providing a combined team of 51 members from 425 (Alouette) Sqn. at Bagotville (five aircraft, 5 pilots, maintenance and weapons load personnel), and six North Bay weapons controllers from the Canadian NORAD Region.

History repeats itself in this fanciful vignette of a CF-18 gun firing pass, drawn for William Tell '86. The target banner has been replaced by a bright red apple; the 20mm cannon by the more traditional crossbow! A disbelieving pilot has some problems of his own to contend with, in the form of minor instrumentation changes. (Louis Mackay)

In a photo finish, the Alouettes were barely nosed out of overall first place by the 33rd TFW, an F-15 team from nearby Eglin AFB, the defending champions. However, they bested eight other teams, including five flying the F-15, and captured more honours than anyone else. Top individual aircrew participant was Capt. John Reed, beating 49 other aircrew in this "best of the best" competition. Reed was a USAF exchange pilot with 425 Sqn. following his six-month CF-18 training course at Cold Lake. The Canadians also had the top aerial gunnery team,

highest score in the live radar missile profile and an intensely fought first place win as most efficient weapons load crew,

425 Sqn. aircraft are readied for flight under the watchful eye of a line judge. The yellow foam rubber nose cap seen on the Sidewinder missile in the foreground prevents damage to the sensitive missile seeker head during ground handling.

Two AIM-9L Sidewinders and two AIM-7 Sparrow missiles await the static weapons load competition in the early morning of Saturday, October 18. (M. Valenti)

led by Sgt. Dave Lavich. Commenting on the surprising success in the gun profile which clinched second place for 425 Sqn., Capt. Reed credits the airplane. "I feel the CF-18 turns a little better than the F-15 because it is a little smaller. We also had a good team strategy. We wanted everybody scoring well to be in a good position. If it came down to guns, we figured we could do as well as anybody..., even without practice."

The five separate flight profiles provided competition under near combat conditions. Profiles I and II were combined into one flight during which the pilot is guided by ground controllers to intercept a maneuvering QF-100 and fire Sparrow and Sidewinder missiles. This competition emphasizes systems and radar function rather than pilot proficiency alone.

Profile III involved a two fighter scramble intercept on two "intruders." The two competition pilots had ten minutes to get airborne, and an additional five and a half minutes to find and perform a VID on the F-16 or F-106 targets, passing close enough to distinguish their tail and wingtip colours. Each interceptor simulated firing two missiles at the bogies.

Entire teams participated in Profile IV. As an air defence exercise, the four team competitors had to defend their allotted airspace for 45 minutes against 12 raiders. Each defending aircraft was limited to three simulated missile shots. To confuse matters, assorted "friendlies" were also in the air, and the raiders employed electronic countermeasures, chaff and jamming.

Pilot members of the high-scoring Canadian Forces William Tell '86 team. Left to right: Capt. Marcel Major, team leader Maj. Mike Stacey, Capt. Chris Hadfield, Capt. John Reed (USAF) and Capt. Pete Van Langenhove.

Profile V evaluated marksmanship using the 20mm gun against an acoustically-scored towed target. This orange-coloured 17 foot piece of elusiveness had to be hit in two separate ways. First, in the shortest possible time, and then fired on to score the most hits from a gun tracking shot. Both events flown by two aircraft as a team must be completed within a 50 second time limit.

The strong finish was both a credit to the skill and determination of aircrew and groundcrew alike, and yet another affirmation of the wisdom of Canada's CF-18 choice. Not only is the spirit of competition strong at William Tell, but so too is the sharing of concepts and tactics, in the quest for better ways and procedures.

"Most people did not credit us with being a good rival for the F-15..." said 425 Sqn. commander LCol. Jean-Michel Comtois. "In fact, it was a two-horse race. This single event has done more for our fighter community's credibility than any other activity we've been involved with in recent years. Our performance has proven us a force to be reckoned with..."

Along with live missile shoots, CF-18s participate on a regular basis at "Flag" exercises. These include deployments to the USAF Copper Flag (electronic warfare/air defence), the well-established Red Flag in the Nevada desert (tactical training), and Maple Flag held twice annually at Cold Lake.

Although 1 CAG's conversion to the Hornet in Europe is still recent, the aircraft is quickly establishing itself in its rightful commanding position within the NATO alliance. A requirement to assess CF-18 compatibility with operational and support facilities throughout NATO resulted in a fall 1986 four-ship deployment to Andoya, Norway in "Fiord Hornet." Additionally, there have been DACT and air-to-air firing exercises with NATO neighbours, as well as flare and chaff effectiveness trials.

Exercise Maple Flag XVII. A CF-18 dual blasts off in front of the AETE hangar at Cold Lake, May 16, 1986. (M. Valenti)

LOOKING AHEAD

While a formalized follow-on purchase of up to twenty additional CF-18s from McAir has been officially rejected by the government, several initiatives are being explored which may result in a modest supplement to the CF-18 fleet in later years.

Electronic warfare self-protection devices for all CF-18s operating in the high-threat NATO theatre is essential. Aircraft are being fitted with an ALR-67 radar homing and warning receiver, ALQ-126B and ALQ-162 active electronic jammers, as well as the ALE-39 chaff and flare dispensers, for an extra measure of security.

As the CF-18 implementation process becomes complete, the Cold Lake OTS is assuming new and challenging tasks. Along with routine replacement aircrew training, the Fighter Weapons Instructor Course (FWIC) has been re-instituted, a Canadian equivalent of TOPGUN and *the* speciality course for fighter pilots in all matters relating to weapons and tactics. FWIC is not new to the Canadian Forces. Programs of this nature were run for years on the CF-104, CF-5 and CF-101, and the CF-5 program has continued to produce a steady stream of graduates.

Among pilots there is universal acclaim for Canada's new fighter. LCol. John Croll, the all-time top alumnus of the USAF test pilot school at Edwards AFB, has flown more than 35 aircraft types, including at least 20 different fighters for over 4,000 accumulated hours. He performed much of the original AETE weapons clearance work on the CF-18 at Cold Lake, in the

A 1 CAG pilot confers with a Royal Norwegian Air Force sentry at Andoya, September, 1986.

CF-18 holds for a Royal Air Force Tornado during TAM '86.

410 Sqn. artist Jim Belliveau's speculation of how the complete electronic warfare suite of radar warning receiver, jammers, flare and chaff dispensers might affect the CF-18's sleek lines. In reality, installation has been significantly more subtle.

process forming an accurate impression of the Hornet's unique strengths. Whereas the F-15 and F-16 both have a slight thrust-to-weight advantage, "the CF-18 has it all over (them) in terms of maneuverability in the pitch axis" at lower speeds. "I like to call it nose pointing capability; you can generate up to a 40°/second pitch rate and have an unlimited angle of attack (with certain configurations on the aircraft)." In two to three seconds the nose of the airplane can be pointed "at an adversary who might be even 90° off your flightpath. Both the F-15 and F-16 have angle of

attack limitations. In my mind the CF-18 is a much superior dogfighter."

Capt. Bob Wade, the CAF's high-profile CF-18 demonstration pilot for two years, also confirms the low-speed attributes of the design. "The CF-18 has a tremendous advantage in the fighter role as it is much more capable of flying at very low airspeed and very high angles of attack (if required). At air displays, I was able to keep the aircraft over the airfield throughout the whole twelve minute display without the crowd ever losing sight of me." Slow flight could be demonstrated "back to 105 knots, quite often running ground speeds of 80-85 knots with the nose 25-30° relative to the airflow (above the airflow). In an air fight, I can turn faster at slower speeds than the other guy."

As the "new kids on the block," Canada's CF-18s have the vast majority of their service careers ahead of them. If the first five years of operational service are any indication, the future looks bright indeed. As one pilot put it, "If I was asked to exercise the missions I have been trained for, I'd choose the CF-18. I know I'd go into combat with an excellent chance of coming home alive."

Capt. Bob Wade of 410 Sqn. regaled airshow audiences for two seasons. He is holding two very important pieces of flight gear — a Mae West and g suit. (M. Valenti)

Duelling classmates. The first joint CF-5/CF-18 FWIC course was conducted at CFB Cold Lake, spring 1987. This 419 Sqn. CF-5A and 410 Sqn. Hornet close up for the photographer during a climb-out to a DACT session.

SCALE DRAWINGS

CF-18A

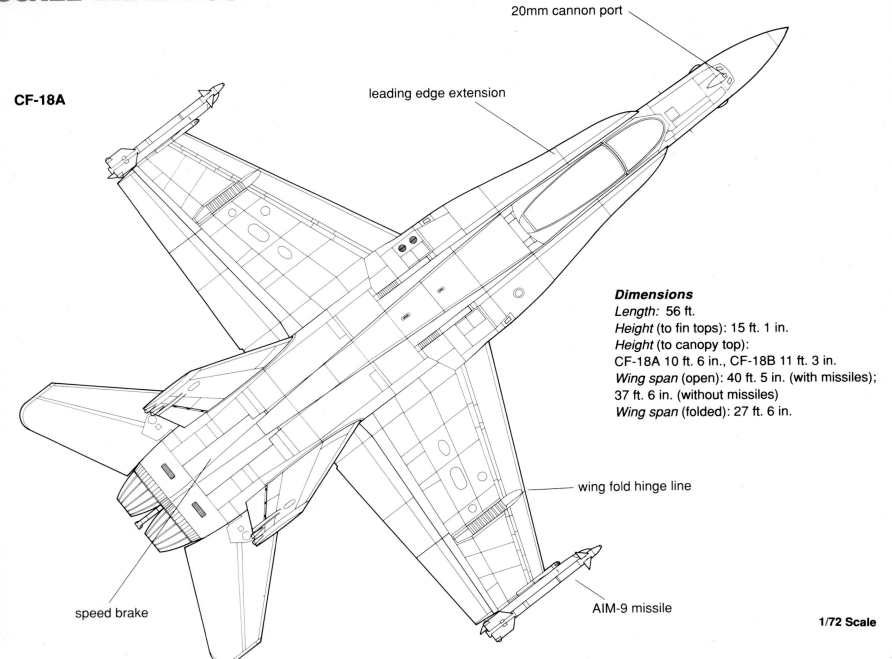

20mm cannon port

leading edge extension

Dimensions
Length: 56 ft.
Height (to fin tops): 15 ft. 1 in.
Height (to canopy top):
CF-18A 10 ft. 6 in., CF-18B 11 ft. 3 in.
Wing span (open): 40 ft. 5 in. (with missiles);
37 ft. 6 in. (without missiles)
Wing span (folded): 27 ft. 6 in.

wing fold hinge line

speed brake

AIM-9 missile

1/72 Scale

Line art by Bob Migliardi

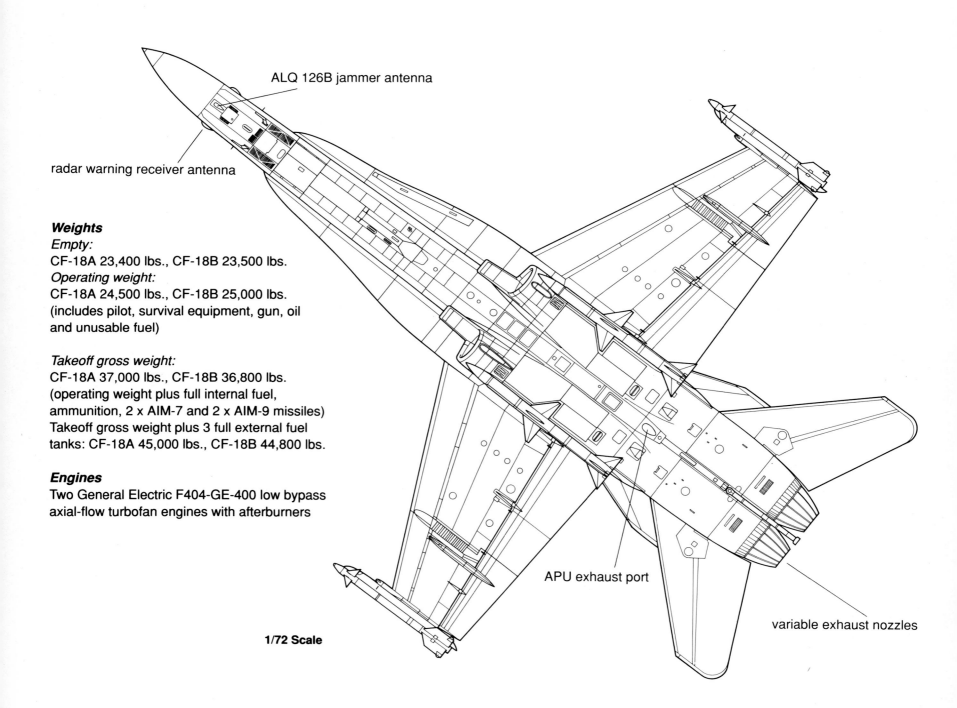

ALQ 126B jammer antenna

radar warning receiver antenna

Weights
Empty:
CF-18A 23,400 lbs., CF-18B 23,500 lbs.
Operating weight:
CF-18A 24,500 lbs., CF-18B 25,000 lbs.
(includes pilot, survival equipment, gun, oil
and unusable fuel)

Takeoff gross weight:
CF-18A 37,000 lbs., CF-18B 36,800 lbs.
(operating weight plus full internal fuel,
ammunition, 2 x AIM-7 and 2 x AIM-9 missiles)
Takeoff gross weight plus 3 full external fuel
tanks: CF-18A 45,000 lbs., CF-18B 44,800 lbs.

Engines
Two General Electric F404-GE-400 low bypass
axial-flow turbofan engines with afterburners

1/72 Scale

APU exhaust port

variable exhaust nozzles

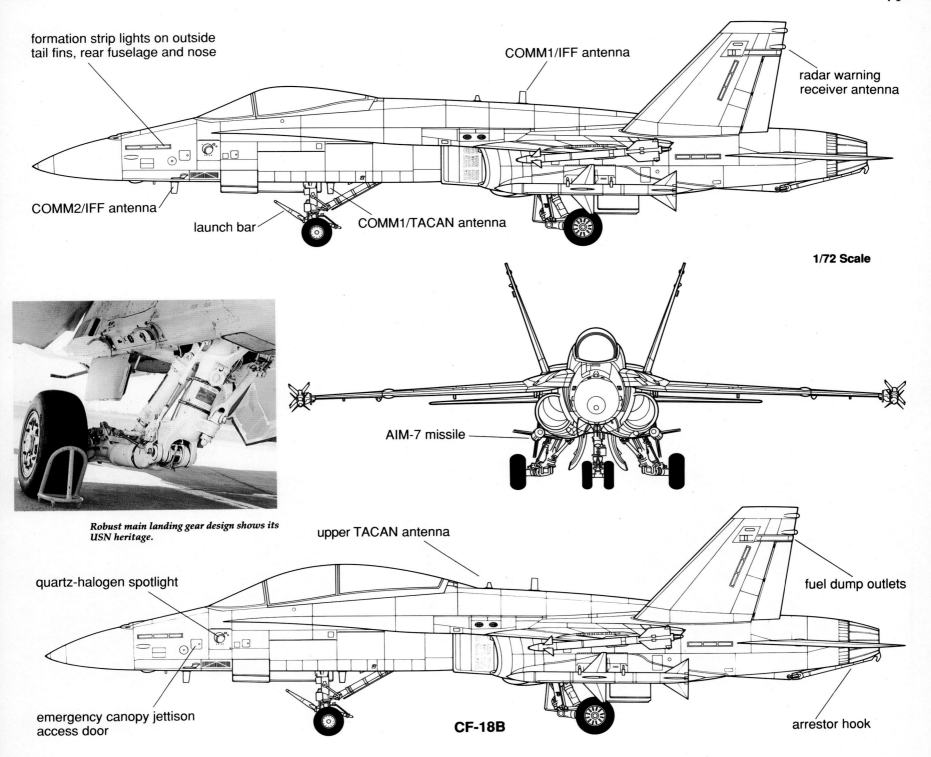

formation strip lights on outside
tail fins, rear fuselage and nose

COMM1/IFF antenna

radar warning
receiver antenna

COMM2/IFF antenna

launch bar

COMM1/TACAN antenna

1/72 Scale

*Robust main landing gear design shows its
USN heritage.*

AIM-7 missile

upper TACAN antenna

quartz-halogen spotlight

fuel dump outlets

emergency canopy jettison
access door

CF-18B

arrestor hook

GLOSSARY

A/A air-to-air
ACM air combat maneuvering
ACMR air combat maneuvering range
ADC air data computer
ADF automatic direction finder
AETE Aerospace Engineering and Test Establishment
A/G air-to-ground
AGL above ground level
AI airborne intercept
AOA *see* angle of attack
analog electronic systems in which quantities are represented by electrical signals which are continuously variable in the relevant characteristics; for example, signal strength.
angels fighter altitude in thousands of feet
angle of attack the angle between the chord line of the wing and the relative wind, presented in degrees.
aspect angle the angle between the line of sight to a target aircraft and the axis of the target aircraft. (If viewed directly tail-on, aspect angle is 0)
ATAF Allied Tactical Air Force
ASL azimuth steering line
AWACS Airborne Warning and Control System
bandit confirmed hostile target
BIT built-in test
BFM basic fighter maneuvers
bogie unidentified airborne target
break a maximum performance defensive turn in which the intensity of the turn is governed by the relative angular position, range and closure of the attacking aircraft.
BS boresight acquisition
BVR beyond visual range
CADIZ Canadian Air Defence Identification Zone
CAG Canadian Air Group
CAP combat air patrol
CAS control augmentation system

CCIP continuously computed impact point
CF Canadian Forces
CFB Canadian Forces Base
CR combat ready
crabbing a landing approach technique in which aircraft heading is offset toward the direction of wind sufficiently to permit the aircraft to fly down the projection of the runway centreline.
DA double attack
DACT dissimilar air combat training
DBS Doppler beam sharpening
DEL direct electrical link
DDI digital display indicator
digital electronic systems in which quantities are represented by patterns or sequences of on-off signals coded to represent numbers.
DIL displayed impact line
Doppler a property of airborne radar that uses the shift in the frequency of signals reflected off the earth's surface ahead of or behind a target aircraft to give measurement of its true groundspeed.
EXP expand
FCC flight control computer
FD flight director mode
Fox One traditional fighter pilot terminology for the launch of a radar-guided missile (AIM-7 Sparrow)
Fox Two the launch of a heat-seeking missile (AIM-9 Sidewinder)
FWIC Fighter Weapons Instructor Course
g a measure of acceleration such that 1g is the acceleration of a body falling freely in the earth's gravity field. Multiples thereof constitute the aircraft's load, or load factor and are read on the cockpit accelerometer or g meter in units.
GCI ground controlled intercept
GUN gun acquisition mode
HACQ HUD acquisition
HI horizontal indicator
HOTAS hands-on-throttle-and-stick
HUD head up display
IFF identification friend-or-foe

IFR instrument flight rules
ILS instrument landing system
INS inertial navigation system
LCR limited combat ready
LEX leading edge extension
MAN manual
MECH mechanical link
MIL military power
MSL mean sea level
NAS Naval Air Station
NATO North Atlantic Treaty Organization
NAV navigation
NFA New Fighter Aircraft
NORAD North American Air Defence
OTS operational training squadron
PRF pulse repetition frequency
pure pursuit an attack curve in which the flight path of the attacker is continuously pointed at the target.
RAID raid assessment
RF radio frequency
ROCC Regional Operations Control Centre
ROE rules of engagement
RWS range-while-search
SEMP Systems Effectiveness Monitoring Program
STT single target track
TA terrain avoidance
TACAN Tactical Air Navigation A navigation and approach aid that provides both bearing and distance to a station.
target aspect *see* aspect angle
TDC throttle designator control
TFS tactical fighter squadron
TWS track-while-scan
UFC up front controller
UHF ultra high frequency
VACQ vertical acquisition
VHF very high frequency
VID visual identification
VOR Very High Frequency Omnidirectional Range A navigation aid which provides a multiple number of courses toward or away from a station.
VS velocity search
VTR video tape recorder
WST weapons system trainer